FRENCH
VISUAL DICTIONARY

Published by Collins
An imprint of HarperCollins Publishers
Westerhill Road
Bishopbriggs
Glasgow G64 2QT

HarperCollins Publishers
1st Floor, Watermarque Building
Ringsend Road, Dublin 4, Ireland

First Edition 2019

10 9 8 7 6 5 4

© HarperCollins Publishers 2019

ISBN 978-0-00-829031-3

Typeset by Jouve, India

Printed in India by Replika Press Pvt. Ltd.

Acknowledgements

We would like to thank those authors and
publishers who kindly gave permission for
copyright material to be used in the Collins
Corpus. We would also like to thank Times
Newspapers Ltd for providing valuable data.

A catalogue record for this book is available
from the British Library

If you would like to comment on any aspect
of this book, please contact us at the given
address or online.
E-mail dictionaries@harpercollins.co.uk
www.facebook.com/collinsdictionary
@collinsdict

MANAGING EDITOR
Maree Airlie

FOR THE PUBLISHER
Gerry Breslin
Gina Macleod
Kevin Robbins
Robin Scrimgeour

CONTRIBUTORS
Maurane Prezelin
Lauren Reid
Emma Thomas

TECHNICAL SUPPORT
Claire Dimeo

MIX
Paper from
responsible sources
FSC™ C007454

CONTENTS

BAKERY AND PATISSERIE | LA BOULANGERIE-PÂTISSERIE

There are strict regulations in place to define what is and isn't a boulangerie in France. Boulangeries must make their bread on-site without preservatives or additives, and cannot freeze the dough or baguettes that they produce for sale.

2 YOU MIGHT SAY...

Do you sell...?
Est-ce que vous avez...?

Could I have...?
Je vais prendre...

How much are...?
À combien sont les...?

3 YOU MIGHT HEAR...

Are you being served?
Est-ce qu'on s'occupe de vous ?

Would you like anything else?
Et avec ceci ?

It costs...
Ça fait...

4 VOCABULARY

baker	slice	flour
le boulanger /	une tranche	la farine
la boulangère		
	crust	gluten-free
bread	la croûte	sans gluten
le pain		
	dough	to bake
loaf	la pâte	faire cuire au four
un pain		

5 YOU SHOULD KNOW...

A "dépôt de pain" is a shop or counter that sells bakery products that have been baked off-site.

1
almond croissant
le croissant aux amandes

baguette
la baguette

bread rolls
les petits pains *mpl*

Whether you're on holiday or staying in a French-speaking country for a slightly longer period of time, your **Collins Visual Dictionary** is designed to help you find exactly what you need, when you need it. With over a thousand clear and helpful images, you can quickly locate the vocabulary you are looking for.

The Visual Dictionary includes:

- 10 **chapters** arranged thematically, so that you can easily find what you need to suit the situation
1. **images** – illustrating essential items
2. **YOU MIGHT SAY...** – common phrases that you might want to use
3. **YOU MIGHT HEAR...** – common phrases that you might come across
4. **VOCABULARY** – common words that you might need
5. **YOU SHOULD KNOW...** – tips about local customs or etiquette
- an **index** to find all images quickly and easily
- essential **phrases** and **numbers** listed on the flaps for quick reference

USING YOUR COLLINS VISUAL DICTIONARY

In order to make sure that the phrases and vocabulary in the **Collins Visual Dictionary** are presented in a way that's clear and easy to understand, we have followed certain policies when translating:

1) The polite form "vous" (you) has been used throughout the text as this is always safe to use, even if a bit formal at times, for example:

> How are you? **Comment allez-vous ?**

Remember that if you are addressing an older person or someone you have just met, you use "vous". However, if you are speaking to children, or those you know well, you can use "tu". French people may invite you to use "tu" with them:

> Shall we call each other "tu"? **On se tutoie ?**

2) The grammatical gender of French nouns has been indicated using the articles "le" (masculine) or "la" (feminine). All nouns which have the article "l'" have been shown with their gender, for example:

> year **l'année** *f*

All plural translations have been marked with the gender of the singular noun, as well as the plural marker, for example:

> trainers **les baskets** *fpl*

Feminine forms of nouns have been shown with the masculine form as the main translation:

> salesperson **le vendeur / la vendeuse**

3) In general, the masculine form of adjectives only has been shown for vocabulary items and in phrases, for example:

> annoyed **mécontent**
>
> I'm tired. **Je suis fatigué.**

However, in some cases both forms are shown:

> I'm married/divorced. (man) **Je suis marié / divorcé.**
> I'm married/divorced. (woman) **Je suis mariée / divorcée.**

Remember that, in French, the adjective often changes depending on whether the noun it describes is masculine or feminine. Often the adjective only adds an "e" to the end, so "content" becomes "contente" and "fatigué" becomes "fatiguée". However, there are some adjectives that take different endings in the feminine form, or don't change at all.

The adjective form also changes if you are talking about a person or object in the singular or in the plural. Usually, the plural form of the adjective is formed by adding "-s" (for masculine nouns) or "-es" (for feminine nouns) to the end of the word.

> The girls are tired. **Les filles sont fatiguées.**

FREE AUDIO

We have created a free audio resource to help you learn and practise the French words for all of the images shown in this dictionary. The French words in each chapter are spoken by native speakers, giving you the opportunity to listen to each word twice and repeat it yourself. Download the audio from the website below to learn all of the vocabulary you need for communicating in French.

www.collinsdictionary.com/resources

QUIZLET

Collins and Quizlet have teamed up to bring you expert-created digital learning resources like pre-made flashcards, quizzes and games to help you master the vocabulary shown in **Collins French Visual Dictionary**. Quickly learn the vocabulary with one of Quizlet's seven different study modes. Visit **quizlet.info/collins-french** to see why 50 million students and teachers use Quizlet each month.

Whether you're going to be visiting a French-speaking country, or even living there, you'll want to be able to chat with people and get to know them better. Being able to communicate effectively with acquaintances, friends, family, and colleagues is key to becoming more confident in French in a variety of everyday situations.

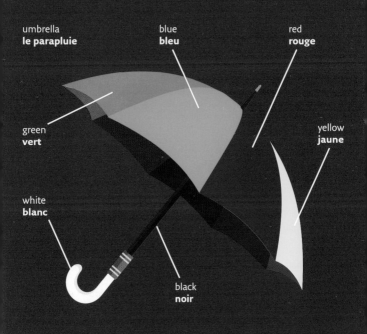

umbrella
le parapluie

blue
bleu

red
rouge

green
vert

yellow
jaune

white
blanc

black
noir

Hello.
Bonjour.

Good evening.
Bonsoir.

See you tomorrow.
À demain.

Hi!
Salut !

Good night.
Bonne nuit.

See you on Saturday.
À samedi.

Hello again!
Rebonjour !

Goodbye.
Au revoir.

Have a good day!
Bonne journée !

Good morning.
Bonjour.

Bye!
Salut !

Have a good evening!
Bonne soirée !

Good afternoon.
Bonjour.

See you soon.
À bientôt.

YOU SHOULD KNOW...

French people are quite formal when initially introduced, shaking hands upon meeting and parting. Friends and relatives will often greet each other with a kiss on the cheek: usually two, but sometimes three, or even four, depending on which region you're in. "Bonjour" is used to greet someone; "bonne journée" is used when taking your leave.

Yes.
Oui / Si.

Thank you.
Merci.

I'm sorry.
Je suis désolé.

No.
Non.

No, thanks.
Non merci.

OK!
D'accord !

I don't know.
Je ne sais pas.

Excuse me.
Excusez-moi.

You're welcome.
De rien.

please
s'il vous plaît

Sorry?
Pardon ?

I don't understand.
Je ne comprends pas.

YOU SHOULD KNOW...

"Oui" or "si"? French has two words for "yes" – you use "oui" when answering an affirmative question, and "si" when responding to a negative one.

"Madame" and "Mademoiselle" can be translated as "Mrs/Ms" and "Miss" respectively. "Mademoiselle" is less frequently used nowadays and tends to be used for young girls rather than adults; "Madame" can refer to a married or an unmarried woman. It's polite to use someone's title when addressing them or trying to get their attention.

How old are you?
Quel âge avez-vous ?

May I ask how old you are?
Puis-je demander votre âge ?

When is your birthday?
Quelle est votre date d'anniversaire ?

I'm ... years old.
J'ai ... ans.

My birthday is on...
Mon anniversaire est le...

Where are you from?
D'où venez-vous ?

Where do you live?
Où habitez-vous ?

I'm from...
Je viens...

... the UK.
... du Royaume-Uni.

I live in...
J'habite à...

I'm...
Je suis...

Scottish
écossais

English
anglais

Irish
irlandais

Welsh
gallois

British
britannique

Are you married?
(to a man)
Êtes-vous marié ?

Are you married?
(to a woman)
Êtes-vous mariée ?

Are you single?
Êtes-vous célibataire ?

I'm married/divorced.
(man)
Je suis marié / divorcé.

I'm married/divorced.
(woman)
Je suis mariée / divorcée.

I have a partner.
J'ai un compagnon / une compagne.

I'm single.
Je suis célibataire.

I'm widowed. (man)
Je suis veuf.

I'm widowed. (woman)
Je suis veuve.

Do you have any children?
Avez-vous des enfants ?

I have ... children.
J'ai ... enfants.

I don't have any children.
Je n'ai pas d'enfants.

FAMILY AND FRIENDS | LA FAMILLE ET LES AMIS

This is my...
Voici mon / ma...

These are my...
Voici mes...

husband
le mari

wife
l'épouse *f*

son
le fils

daughter
la fille

parents
les parents *mpl*

partner
**le compagnon /
la compagne**

boyfriend
le copain

girlfriend
la copine

fiancé/fiancée
le fiancé / la fiancée

father
le père

mother
la mère

brother
le frère

sister
la sœur

grandfather
le grand-père

grandmother
la grand-mère

grandson
le petit-fils

granddaughter
la petite-fille

father-in-law/
stepfather
le beau-père

mother-in-law/
stepmother
la belle-mère

daughter-in-law/
stepdaughter
la belle-fille

son-in-law/stepson
le beau-fils

brother-in-law/
stepbrother
le beau-frère

sister-in-law/
stepsister
la belle-sœur

uncle
l'oncle *m*

aunt
la tante

nephew
le neveu

niece
la nièce

cousin
**le cousin /
la cousine**

friend
l'ami *m* **/ l'amie** *f*

colleague
**le collègue /
la collègue**

neighbour
**le voisin /
la voisine**

baby
le bébé

child
l'enfant *m*

teenager
l'adolescent *m* **/
l'adolescente** *f*

How are you?
Comment allez-vous ?

How's it going?
Comment ça va ?

How is he/she?
Comment va-t-il / elle ?

How are they?
Comment vont-ils / elles ?

Very well, thanks, and you?
Très bien, merci, et vous ?

Fine, thanks.
Bien, merci.

Great!
Super bien !

So-so.
Comme ci comme ça.

Not bad, thanks.
Pas mal, merci.

Could be worse.
On fait aller.

Not great.
Pas terrible.

I'm tired.
Je suis fatigué.

I'm hungry/thirsty.
J'ai faim / soif.

I'm full.
Je n'ai plus faim.

I'm cold.
J'ai froid.

I'm warm.
J'ai chaud.

I am...
Je suis...

He/She is...
Il / Elle est...

They are...
Ils / Elles sont...

happy
heureux

excited
excité

calm
calme

surprised
surpris

annoyed
mécontent

angry
en colère

sad
triste

worried
inquiet

afraid
effrayé

relaxed
détendu

I'm bored.
Je m'ennuie.

I feel...
Je me sens...

He/She feels...
Il / Elle se sent...

They feel...
Ils / Elles se sentent...

well
bien

unwell
indisposé

better
mieux

worse
pire

Where do you work?
Où travaillez-vous ?

What do you do?
Que faites-vous dans la vie ?

What's your occupation?
Quel est votre métier ?

Do you work/study?
Est-ce que vous travaillez / étudiez ?

I'm self-employed.
Je travaille à mon compte.

I'm unemployed.
Je suis au chômage.

I'm still at school.
Je suis encore à l'école.

I'm at university.
Je suis à l'université.

I'm retired.
Je suis à la retraite.

I'm travelling.
Je voyage.

I work from home.
Je travaille de chez moi.

I work part-/full-time.
Je travaille à temps partiel / complet.

I work as a/an...
Je travaille comme...

I'm a/an...
Je suis...

architect
l'architecte *m* /
l'architecte *f*

chef
le chef / la chef

civil servant
**le fonctionnaire /
la fonctionnaire**

cleaner
l'employé de ménage *m* /
l'employée de ménage *f*

dentist
**le dentiste /
la dentiste**

doctor
**le médecin /
la médecin**

driver
**le conducteur /
la conductrice**

electrician
l'électricien *m* /
l'électricienne *f*

engineer
l'ingénieur *m* /
l'ingénieure *f*

farmer
l'agriculteur *m* /
l'agricultrice *f*

firefighter
**le sapeur-pompier /
la sapeur-pompier**

fisherman
**le pêcheur /
la pêcheuse**

IT worker
l'informaticien *m* /
l'informaticienne *f*

joiner
**le menuisier /
la menuisière**

journalist
**le journaliste /
la journaliste**

lawyer
l'avocat *m* /
l'avocate *f*

mechanic
**le mécanicien /
la mécanicienne**

nurse
l'infirmier *m* /
l'infirmière *f*

office worker
l'employé de bureau *m* / **l'employée de bureau** *f*

plumber
**le plombier /
la plombière**

police officer
**le policier /
la policière**

postal worker
le facteur / la factrice

sailor
**le marin /
la femme marin**

salesperson
**le vendeur /
la vendeuse**

scientist
**le scientifique /
la scientifique**

soldier
le soldat / la soldate

teacher
**le professeur /
la professeure**

vet
**le vétérinaire /
la vétérinaire**

waiter
le serveur

waitress
la serveuse

I work at/for/in...
**Je travaille à / pour /
dans...**

business
le commerce

company
la compagnie

construction site
le chantier

factory
l'usine *f*

government
le gouvernement

hospital
l'hôpital *m*

hotel
l'hôtel *m*

office
le bureau

restaurant
le restaurant

school
l'école *f*

shop
le magasin

YOU SHOULD KNOW...

When talking about somebody's occupation in French, you do not translate "a", for example "Elle est professeure" – "She's a teacher".

English	What time is it?	When...?
morning **le matin**	**What time is it?** **Quelle heure est-il ?**	**When...?** **Quand...?**

morning
le matin

afternoon
l'après-midi *m*

evening
le soir

night
la nuit

midday
le midi

midnight
minuit *m*

today
aujourd'hui

tonight
ce soir

tomorrow
demain

yesterday
hier

a.m.
du matin

p.m.
**de l'après-midi /
du soir**

What time is it?
Quelle heure est-il ?

It's nine o'clock.
Il est neuf heures.

It's ten past nine.
Il est neuf heures dix.

It's quarter past nine.
**Il est neuf heures
et quart.**

It's 25 past nine.
**Il est neuf heures
vingt-cinq.**

It's half past nine.
**Il est neuf heures
et demie.**

It's 20 to ten.
**Il est dix heures
moins vingt.**

It's quarter to ten.
**Il est dix heures
moins le quart.**

It's five to ten.
**Il est dix heures
moins cinq.**

It's 17:30.
**Il est dix-sept
heures trente.**

When...?
Quand...?

... in 60 seconds/
two minutes.
**... dans 60 secondes /
deux minutes.**

... in quarter of an
hour/half an hour/an
hour.
**... dans un quart
d'heure / une demi-
heure / une heure.**

early
tôt

late
tard

soon
bientôt

later
plus tard

now
maintenant

before
avant

after
après

YOU SHOULD KNOW...

In France – and across Europe – it's more common to use the 24-hour clock.
Remember that quarter past, half past, and quarter to use numbers ("quinze",
"trente" and "quarante-cinq") in this case.

Monday **lundi**	Wednesday **mercredi**	Friday **vendredi**	Sunday **dimanche**
Tuesday **mardi**	Thursday **jeudi**	Saturday **samedi**	

January **janvier**	April **avril**	July **juillet**	October **octobre**
February **février**	May **mai**	August **août**	November **novembre**
March **mars**	June **juin**	September **septembre**	December **décembre**

day **le jour**	fortnightly **tous les quinze jours**	in February **en février**
weekend **le week-end**	monthly **mensuel**	in 2019 **en 2019**
week **la semaine**	yearly **annuel**	in the '80s **dans les années 80**
fortnight **les quinze jours** *mpl*	on Mondays **les lundis**	spring **le printemps**
month **le mois**	every Sunday **tous les dimanches**	summer **l'été** *m*
year **l'année** *f*	last Thursday **jeudi dernier**	autumn **l'automne** *m*
decade **la décennie**	next Friday **vendredi prochain**	winter **l'hiver** *m*
daily **quotidien**	the week before **la semaine d'avant**	in spring **au printemps**
weekly **hebdomadaire**	the week after **la semaine d'après**	in winter **en hiver**

How's the weather?
Quel temps fait-il ?

What's the forecast for
today/tomorrow?
**Quelles sont les
prévisons météo
pour aujourd'hui /
demain ?**

How warm/cold is it?
**Est-ce qu'il fait
chaud / froid ?**

Is it going to rain?
**Est-ce qu'il va
pleuvoir ?**

What a lovely day!
**Quelle belle
journée !**

What awful weather!
**Quel mauvais
temps !**

It's sunny.
Il y a du soleil.

It's cloudy/misty.
**C'est nuageux /
brumeux.**

It's foggy.
Il y a du brouillard.

It's freezing.
Il gèle.

It's raining/snowing.
Il pleut / neige.

It's windy.
Il y a du vent.

It's stormy.
Il y a de l'orage.

It's changeable.
**Le temps est
changeant.**

It is...
Il fait...

nice
beau

horrible
mauvais

hot
chaud

warm
chaud

mild
doux

cool
frais

wet
pluvieux

humid
humide

sun
le soleil

rain
la pluie

snow
la neige

hail
la grêle

wind
le vent

gale
le coup de vent

mist
la brume

fog
le brouillard

thunder
le tonnerre

lightning
l'éclair *m*

thunderstorm
l'orage *m*

cloud
le nuage

temperature
la température

TRANSPORT | LES TRANSPORTS

Travelling to and around France has never been easier. You can travel to France from the UK by air, sea, and rail (thanks to the Channel Tunnel). France's railway system boasts some of the fastest passenger trains in the world – it can be quicker to travel by train than by plane between certain cities – and the country is well connected by road. Local public transport is widely developed and Paris is famous for its métro, one of the oldest underground rail services in the world.

helicopter
l'hélicoptère *m*

rotor
le rotor

blade
la pale

cockpit
le cockpit

nose
le nez

tail
la queue

When asking for directions, it's easiest simply to state your destination, followed by "s'il vous plaît". It's always most polite to use "Monsieur" or "Madame" to address any passers-by you stop and ask.

YOU MIGHT SAY...

Excuse me...
Excusez-moi...

Where is...?
Où se trouve...?

Which way is...?
C'est par où, ...?

What's the quickest way to...?
Quel est le chemin le plus rapide pour...?

How far away is it?
C'est à quelle distance ?

Is it far from here?
C'est loin ?

I'm lost.
Je suis perdu.

I'm looking for...
Je cherche...

I'm going to...
Je vais à...

Can I walk there?
Je peux y aller à pied ?

YOU MIGHT HEAR...

It's over there.
C'est là-bas.

It's in the other direction.
C'est dans l'autre direction.

It's ... metres/minutes away.
C'est à ... mètres / minutes d'ici.

Go straight ahead.
Continuez tout droit.

Turn left/right.
Tournez à gauche / droite.

It's next to...
C'est à côté de...

It's opposite...
C'est en face de...

It's near to...
C'est près de...

Follow the signs for...
Prenez la direction...

street la rue	rush hour l'heure de pointe *f*	road sign le panneau de signalisation
driver le conducteur / la conductrice	public transport les transports en commun *mpl*	to walk marcher
passenger le passager / la passagère	taxi le taxi	to drive conduire
pedestrian le piéton / la piétonne	taxi rank la station de taxis	to return revenir
	directions les indications *fpl*	to cross traverser
traffic le trafic	route l'itinéraire *m*	to turn tourner
traffic jam l'embouteillage *m*		to commute faire la navette

YOU SHOULD KNOW...

At pedestrian crossings, be aware that traffic lights will go straight from red to green, without an amber light to signal a change.

map
la carte

ticket
le billet

timetable
l'horaire *m*

Traffic drives on the right-hand side in France. Remember to carry your ID, driving licence, insurance, and car registration documents with you while driving.

YOU MIGHT SAY...

Is this the road to...?
C'est la route pour...?

Can I park here?
Je peux me garer ici ?

Do I have to pay to park?
Est-ce que le parking est payant ?

I'd like a taxi to...
Je voudrais un taxi pour aller à...

I'd like to hire a car...
J'aimerais louer une voiture...

... for 4 days/a week.
... pour 4 jours / une semaine.

What is your daily rate?
Quel est votre prix à la journée ?

When/Where must I return it?
Quand / Où est-ce que je dois la rendre ?

Where is the nearest petrol station?
Où est la station-service la plus proche ?

I'd like ... euros/litres of fuel, please.
J'aimerais avoir ... euros / litres d'essence, s'il vous plaît.

YOU MIGHT HEAR...

You can/can't park here.
Vous pouvez / ne pouvez pas vous garer ici.

It's free to park here.
Le parking est gratuit ici.

It costs ... to park here.
Ça coûte ... de se garer ici.

Car hire is ... per day/week.
La location de voiture est à ... par jour / semaine.

May I see your documents, please?
Vos papiers, s'il vous plaît.

Please return it to...
Rendez-la à ..., s'il vous plaît.

Please return the car with a full tank of fuel.
Veuillez rendre la voiture avec le plein d'essence.

Which pump are you at?
Vous êtes à quelle pompe ?

How much fuel would you like?
Combien d'essence voulez-vous ?

people carrier
le monospace

SUV
le SUV

motorhome
le camping-car

caravan
la caravane

convertible
la décapotable

passenger seat
le siège du passager

driver's seat
la place du conducteur

back seat
le siège arrière

child seat
le siège enfant

roof rack
la galerie

sunroof
le toit ouvrant

engine
le moteur

battery
la batterie

brake
le frein

accelerator
l'accélérateur *m*

air conditioning
la climatisation

clutch
l'embrayage *m*

cruise control
le régulateur de vitesse

exhaust (pipe)
le pot d'échappement

fuel tank
le réservoir de carburant

gearbox
la boîte de vitesses

Breathalyser®
l'alcootest *m*

automatic
automatique

electric
électrique

hybrid
hybride

to start the engine
démarrer

to brake
freiner

to overtake
dépasser

to park
garer

to reverse
faire marche arrière

to slow down
ralentir

to speed
être en excès de vitesse

to stop
s'arrêter

YOU SHOULD KNOW...

Sat navs that are able to detect speed cameras are illegal in France, so take care to disable this option if you wish to use your sat nav while driving.

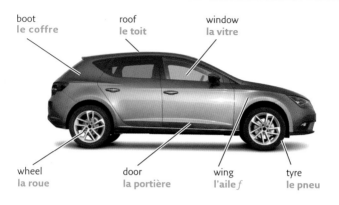

boot
le coffre

roof
le toit

window
la vitre

wheel
la roue

door
la portière

wing
l'aile *f*

tyre
le pneu

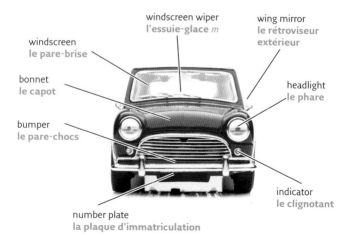

windscreen wiper
l'essuie-glace *m*

wing mirror
**le rétroviseur
extérieur**

windscreen
le pare-brise

bonnet
le capot

headlight
le phare

bumper
le pare-chocs

indicator
le clignotant

number plate
la plaque d'immatriculation

dashboard
le tableau de bord

fuel gauge
la jauge d'essence

gear stick
le levier de vitesse

glove compartment
la boîte à gants

handbrake
le frein à main

headrest
l'appuie-tête *m*

ignition
l'allumage *m*

rearview mirror
le rétroviseur

sat nav
le GPS

seatbelt
la ceinture de sécurité

speedometer
le compteur de vitesse

steering wheel
le volant

France has an excellent motorway system, but be aware that many of the "autoroutes" are toll-paying. Where possible, avoid motorway travel on "Black Saturdays" ("samedis noirs") – these are periods of dense road traffic that occur at the beginning of French holiday times.

VOCABULARY

dual carriageway
la route à quatre voies

single-track road
la route à voie unique

tarmac®
le macadam

corner
le coin

exit
la sortie

slip road
la bretelle

layby
le bas-côté

services
l'aire de service *f*

speed limit
la limitation de vitesse

diversion
la déviation

driving licence
le permis de conduire

car registration document
la carte grise

car insurance
l'assurance automobile *f*

car hire/rental
la location de voiture

unleaded petrol
l'essence sans plomb *f*

diesel
le diesel

roadworks
les travaux *mpl*

YOU SHOULD KNOW...

Speed limits on French roads go by kmph, not mph. In dry weather, the limits are 50 kmph (31 mph) in built-up areas; 80 kmph (49 mph) on two-lane highways; 110 kmph (68 mph) on dual carriageways; and 130 kmph (80 mph) on motorways. In wet weather, the limit is reduced by 20 kmph on motorways, and by 10 kmph on any other roads.

accessible parking space
la place de parking handicapé

bridge
le pont

car park
le parking

car wash
la station de lavage

fuel pump
la pompe à essence

junction
le carrefour

kerb
le bord du trottoir

lane
la voie

level crossing
le passage à niveau

motorway
l'autoroute *f*

parking meter
le parcmètre

parking space
la place de parking

pavement
le trottoir

petrol station
la station-service

pothole
le nid-de-poule

road
la route

roundabout
le rond-point

speed camera
le radar

toll point
le péage

traffic cone
**le cône de
signalisation**

traffic lights
les feux *mpl*

traffic warden
**l'agent de la
circulation** *m/f*

tunnel
le tunnel

zebra crossing
le passage piéton

If you break down on the motorway, call the police or the breakdown service operating in that area using one of the orange emergency telephones that are located every 2 km along the side of the road. Otherwise, call 112 to contact the emergency services.

YOU MIGHT SAY...

Can you help me?
Pouvez-vous m'aider ?

I've broken down.
Je suis tombé en panne.

I've had an accident.
J'ai eu un accident.

I've run out of petrol.
J'ai une panne d'essence.

I've got a flat tyre.
J'ai un pneu crevé.

I've lost my car keys.
J'ai perdu mes clés de voiture.

The car won't start.
La voiture ne démarre pas.

There's a problem with...
Il y a un problème avec...

I've been injured.
Je suis blessé.

Call an ambulance/the police.
Appelez les secours / la police.

Can you send a breakdown van?
Pouvez-vous m'envoyer une dépanneuse ?

Is there a garage/petrol station nearby?
Est-ce qu'il y a un garage / une station-service près d'ici ?

Can you tow me to a garage?
Pouvez-vous me remorquer jusqu'au garage ?

Can you help me change this wheel?
Pouvez-vous m'aider à changer la roue ?

How much will a repair cost?
Combien coûte la réparation ?

When will the car be fixed?
Quand la voiture sera-t-elle réparée ?

May I take your insurance details?
Pouvez-vous me donner les coordonnées de votre assureur ?

Do you need any help?
Vous avez besoin d'aide ?

Are you hurt?
Vous êtes blessé ?

What's wrong with your car?
Qu'est-ce qui ne va pas avec votre voiture ?

Where have you broken down?
Où êtes-vous tombé en panne ?

I can tow you to...
Je peux vous remorquer jusqu'à...

I can give you a jumpstart.
Je peux la faire démarrer avec des câbles.

The repairs will cost...
Les réparations vous coûteront...

We need to order new parts.
On doit commander de nouvelles pièces.

The car will be ready by...
La voiture sera prête à...

I need to take your insurance details.
J'ai besoin des coordonnées de votre assureur.

VOCABULARY

accident	flat tyre	to have a flat tyre
l'accident *m*	**le pneu à plat**	**avoir un pneu à plat**
breakdown	to break down	to change a tyre
la panne	**tomber en panne**	**changer le pneu**
collision	to have an accident	to tow
la collision	**avoir un accident**	**remorquer**

YOU SHOULD KNOW...

When driving in France, you are legally required to have the following in your car: headlight converters; spare bulbs; warning triangles; hi-viz vests; and a Breathalyser® kit. You must also display a GB car sticker if you are driving a UK-registered vehicle.

airbag
l'airbag *m*

antifreeze
l'antigel *m*

emergency phone
la borne d'urgence

garage
le garage

hi-viz vest
le gilet de sécurité

jack
le cric

jump leads
les câbles de
démarrage *mpl*

mechanic
le mécanicien /
la mécanicienne

snow chains
les chaînes à neige
fpl

spare wheel
la roue de secours

tow truck
la dépanneuse

warning triangle
le triangle de
présignalisation

Local bus services are often well organized and useful; for longer journeys, rail services are usually faster and more frequent than bus or coach services.

YOU MIGHT SAY...

Is there a bus to...?
Est-ce qu'il y a un bus pour...?

When is the next bus to...?
Quand part le prochain bus pour...?

Which bus goes to the city centre?
Quel bus faut-il prendre pour aller au centre-ville ?

Where is the bus stop?
Où est l'arrêt de bus ?

Which stand does the coach leave from?
De quel quai ce car part-il ?

Where can I buy tickets?
Où est-ce que je peux acheter des tickets de bus ?

How much is it to go to...?
Combien ça coûte pour aller à...?

A full/half fare, please.
Un ticket au plein tarif / tarif réduit, s'il vous plaît.

A single/return.
Un aller simple / aller-retour.

Could you tell me when to get off?
Pouvez-vous me dire quand je dois descendre ?

How many stops is it?
C'est dans combien d'arrêts ?

I want to get off at the next stop, please.
Je veux descendre au prochain arrêt, s'il vous plaît.

YOU MIGHT HEAR...

The number 17 goes to...
La ligne 17 va à...

The bus stop is...
L'arrêt de bus est...

It leaves from stand 21.
Il part du quai 21.

There's a bus every 10 minutes.
Il y a un bus toutes les 10 minutes.

You buy tickets at the machine/office.
Vous pouvez acheter des tickets au distributeur / à l'agence.

This is your stop, sir/madam.
C'est votre arrêt, Monsieur / Madame.

bus route	full fare	school bus
la ligne de bus	**le plein tarif**	**le car de ramassage scolaire**
bus lane	half fare	
la voie réservée aux bus	**le demi-tarif**	airport bus
		la navette de l'aéroport
	concession	
bus station	**la réduction**	tour bus
la gare routière		**l'autocar touristique** *m*
	wheelchair access	
bus pass	**l'accessibilité aux handicapés** *f*	
la carte de bus		to catch the bus
		prendre le bus
fare	night bus	
le prix	**le bus de nuit**	

You may be required to validate ("composter") your ticket as you board your bus.

bus	bus shelter	bus stop
le bus	**l'Abribus®** *m*	**l'arrêt de bus** *m*

coach	minibus	trolley bus
le car	**le minibus**	**le trolleybus**

There are plenty of cycling routes in France, both short- and long-distance. The green "Accueil Vélo"© logo indicates where facilities and information are available for cyclists.

YOU MIGHT SAY...

Where can I hire a bicycle?
Où est-ce que je peux louer des vélos ?

My bike is damaged/has a puncture.
Mon vélo est abîmé / a crevé.

How much is it to hire?
Combien coûte la location ?

YOU MIGHT HEAR...

Bike hire is ... per day/week.
La location de vélo est à ... par jour / par semaine.

You must wear a helmet.
Vous devez porter un casque.

VOCABULARY

cyclist **le cycliste / la cycliste**	bike rack **le porte-vélos**	to cycle **faire du vélo**
mountain bike **le VTT**	cycle lane/path **la piste cyclable**	to go for a bike ride **faire une promenade en vélo**
road bike **le vélo de route**	reflective vest **le gilet de sécurité**	to get a puncture **crever**
bike stand **le râtelier à bicyclettes**	child seat **le siège enfant**	
	puncture repair kit **la trousse crevaison**	

YOU SHOULD KNOW...

France hosts the world-famous cycling road race, the Tour de France.

ACCESSORIES

bell
la sonnette

bike lock
l'antivol *m*

front light
le phare avant

helmet
le casque

pump
la pompe à vélo

reflector
le réflecteur

BICYCLE

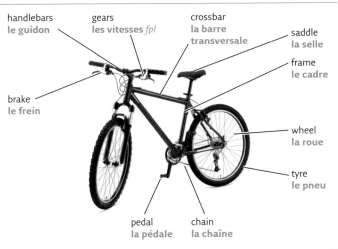

handlebars
le guidon

gears
les vitesses *fpl*

crossbar
la barre transversale

saddle
la selle

frame
le cadre

brake
le frein

wheel
la roue

tyre
le pneu

pedal
la pédale

chain
la chaîne

VOCABULARY

motorcyclist
**le motard /
la motarde**

moped
la mobylette

scooter
le scooter

fuel tank
**le réservoir
de carburant**

handlebars
le guidon

mudguard
le garde-boue

kickstand
la béquille

exhaust pipe
**le tuyau
d'échappement**

leathers
**les vêtements de
moto** *mpl*

YOU SHOULD KNOW...

Motorcyclists must wear hi-viz clothing and have reflective elements on their helmets.

boots
les bottes *fpl*

helmet
le casque

helmet cam
**la caméra pour
casque**

leather gloves
les gants en cuir *mpl*

leather jacket
le blouson de cuir

motorbike
la moto

France has a well-developed, well-organized national railway system. Before boarding a train, it's important to validate ("composter") your ticket: failure to do so can result in a fine. However, self-printed e-tickets are exempt from this requirement.

YOU MIGHT SAY...

Is there a train to...?
Est-ce qu'il y a un train pour...?

I'd like to reserve a seat, please.
J'aimerais réserver une place, s'il vous plaît.

When is the next train to...?
À quelle heure est le prochain train pour...?

Do I have to change?
Est-ce qu'il y a une correspondance ?

Where is the nearest metro station?
Où est la station de métro la plus proche ?

Where do I change for...?
Où est la correspondance pour...?

Which platform does it leave from?
De quel quai part-il ?

Where is platform 4?
Où est le quai numéro 4 ?

Which line do I take for...?
Quelle ligne dois-je prendre pour...?

Is this the right train/platform for...?
C'est bien le train / quai pour...?

A ticket to ..., please.
Un billet pour ..., s'il vous plaît.

Is this seat free?
Est-ce que ce siège est libre ?

A single/return ticket to ..., please.
Un aller simple / aller-retour pour ..., s'il vous plaît.

I've missed my train!
J'ai raté mon train !

YOU SHOULD KNOW...

The word "metro" is derived from the name of the company that was first set up to operate the Paris network, "La compagnie du chemin de fer métropolitain de Paris". It is now widely used across the world as a name for any underground rail system.

35

The next train leaves at...
Le prochain train part à...

This is the right train/platform.
C'est le bon train / quai.

Would you like a single or return ticket?
Voulez-vous un aller simple ou un aller-retour ?

You have to go to platform 2.
Vous devez aller sur le quai numéro 2.

I'm sorry, this journey is fully booked.
Je suis désolé, ce train est complet.

This seat is free/taken.
Ce siège est / n'est pas libre.

Tickets, please.
Vos billets, s'il vous plaît.

You must change at...
Vous avez une correspondance à...

The next stop is...
Le prochain arrêt est...

Platform 4 is down there.
Le quai numéro 4 est par là.

Change here for...
Descendez ici pour aller à...

VOCABULARY

rail network
le réseau ferroviaire

coach
le wagon

return ticket
l'aller-retour *m*

high-speed train
le train à grande vitesse

metro station
la station de métro

e-ticket
le billet électronique

passenger train
le train de passagers

left luggage
la consigne

first class
la première classe

railcard
la carte de réduction

seat reservation
la réservation

freight train
le train de marchandises

book of tickets
le carnet

to change trains
changer de train

sleeper
le train-couchettes

single ticket
l'aller simple *m*

to validate a ticket
composter un billet

quiet coach
l'espace calme *m*

carriage
le wagon

couchette
la couchette

departure board
le tableau des départs

guard
le garde / la garde

light railway
le TLR

locomotive
la locomotive

luggage rack
le porte-bagages

metro
le métro

platform
le quai

porter
le porteur / la porteuse

restaurant car
la voiture-restaurant

sliding doors
la porte coulissante

ticket barrier
le portillon

ticket machine
le guichet automatique

ticket office
le guichet

track
la voie

train
le train

train conductor
le chef de train / la chef de train

tram
le tramway

train station
la gare

validation machine
le composteur de billets

France has many airports, but a number of airlines only operate seasonal routes from the UK to some areas of France, so it is best to check when flights to less central destinations are available.

YOU MIGHT SAY...

I'm looking for check-in/my gate.
Je cherche l'enregistrement /
ma porte d'embarquement.

I'm checking in one case.
J'enregistre une valise.

Which gate does the plane leave from?
De quelle porte part l'avion ?

When does the gate open/close?
À quelle heure l'embarquement commence-t-il / se termine-t-il ?

Is the flight on time?
Ce vol est-il à l'heure ?

I would like a window/an aisle seat, please.
J'aimerais un siège côté hublot / couloir, s'il vous plaît.

I've lost my luggage.
J'ai perdu mes bagages.

My flight has been delayed.
Mon vol a du retard.

I've missed my connecting flight.
J'ai raté ma correspondance.

Is there a shuttle bus service?
Est-ce qu'il y a une navette ?

YOU MIGHT HEAR...

Check-in has opened for flight...
L'enregistrement pour le vol ...
est ouvert.

May I see your passport, please?
Puis-je voir votre passeport, s'il vous plaît ?

How many bags are you checking in?
Combien de bagages enregistrez-vous ?

Your luggage exceeds the maximum weight.
Vos bagages dépassent la limite de poids autorisé.

Please go to gate number...
Veuillez vous diriger vers la porte...

Your flight is on time/delayed.
Votre vol est à l'heure / en retard.

Is this your bag?
C'est votre valise ?

Flight ... is now ready for boarding.
L'embarquement pour le vol ...
va commencer.

Last call for passenger...
Dernier appel pour le passager...

airline
la compagnie aérienne

terminal
le terminal

Arrivals/Departures
Arrivées / Départs

security
les contrôles de sécurité *mpl*

passport control
le contrôle des passeports

customs
la douane

gate
la porte

cabin crew
le personnel navigant

flight attendant
le steward / l'hôtesse *f*

business/economy class
la classe affaires / économique

aisle
le couloir

tray table
la tablette

overhead locker
le compartiment à bagages

seatbelt
la ceinture de sécurité

life jacket
le gilet de sauvetage

oxygen mask
le masque à oxygène

hold
la soute

wing
l'aile *f*

engine
le moteur

fuselage
le fuselage

hold luggage
les bagages enregistrés *mpl*

cabin baggage
les bagages en cabine *mpl*

excess baggage
l'excédent de bagages *m*

hand luggage
le bagage à main

jetlag
le décalage horaire

to check in (online)
s'enregistrer (en ligne)

aeroplane
l'avion *m*

airport
l'aéroport *m*

baggage reclaim
le retrait des bagages

boarding card
**la carte
d'embarquement**

cabin
la cabine

check-in desk
l'enregistrement *m*

cockpit
le cockpit

departure board
**le tableau des
départs**

duty-free shop
**la boutique hors
taxes**

holdall
le sac fourre-tout

luggage trolley
le chariot à bagages

passport
le passeport

pilot
le pilote / la pilote

runway
la piste

suitcase
la valise

There are numerous ferry ports on the northern and southern coasts of France, connecting the country to various European and North African destinations. There is also a well-developed waterway system of rivers and canals roughly 8,500 km long.

YOU MIGHT SAY...

When is the next boat to...?
À quelle heure est le prochain bateau pour...?

Where does the boat leave from?
D'où part ce bateau ?

What time is the last boat to...?
À quelle heure est le dernier bateau pour...?

How long is the trip/crossing?
Combien de temps dure le trajet / la traversée ?

How many crossings a day are there?
Combien y a-t-il de traversées par jour ?

How much for ... passengers?
Combien ça coûte pour ... passagers ?

How much is it for a vehicle?
Combien ça coûte pour une voiture ?

I feel seasick.
J'ai le mal de mer.

YOU MIGHT HEAR...

The boat leaves from...
Le bateau part de...

The trip/crossing lasts...
Le trajet / La traversée dure...

There are ... crossings a day.
Il y a ... traversées par jour.

The ferry is delayed/cancelled.
Le ferry a du retard / est annulé.

Sea conditions are good/bad.
Les conditions en mer sont bonnes / mauvaises.

VOCABULARY

ferry crossing
la traversée en ferry

ferry terminal
le terminal de ferry

car deck
le pont-garage

deck
le pont

porthole
le hublot

funnel
la cheminée

bow
la proue

stern
la poupe

port
le port

marina
le port de plaisance

pier
la jetée

canal
le canal

coastguard
le garde-côte

lifeboat
le canot de sauvetage

captain
le capitaine / la capitaine

crew
l'équipage *m*

foot passenger
le piéton / la piétonne

to board
monter à bord de

to sail
naviguer

to dock
mettre à quai

GENERAL

anchor
l'ancre *f*

buoy
la bouée

gangway
la passerelle

harbour
le port

jetty
la jetée

lifebuoy
la bouée de sauvetage

lifejacket
le gilet de sauvetage

lock
l'écluse *f*

mooring
le mouillage

canal boat
la péniche

canoe
le canoë

ferry
le ferry

inflatable dinghy
le canot pneumatique

kayak
le kayak

liner
le paquebot

rowing boat
la barque

sailing boat
le voilier

yacht
le yacht

France attracts huge numbers of tourists and expats looking for a place to call "chez soi" for a time, whether it's for a holiday or a longer-term stay. This could be a central city apartment, a cosy gîte in a rural spot, or an expansive and luxurious château.

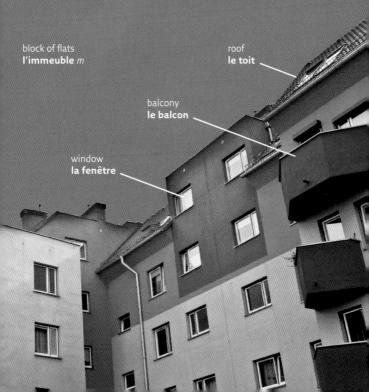

block of flats
l'immeuble *m*

roof
le toit

balcony
le balcon

window
la fenêtre

Most of France's population lives in urban areas, although it's quite common for people to head out of the city for "un week-end au vert" (a weekend in the country), perhaps to see family or explore the countryside.

YOU MIGHT SAY...

I live in...
J'habite à...

I'm staying at...
Je loge à...

My address is...
Mon adresse est...

I have a flat/house.
J'ai un appartement / une maison.

I'm the homeowner/tenant.
Je suis le propriétaire / locataire.

I've recently moved.
Je viens d'emménager.

I'm moving to...
Je déménage à...

I'd like to buy/rent a property here.
J'aimerais acheter / louer ici.

YOU MIGHT HEAR...

Where do you live?
Où habitez-vous ?

Where are you staying?
Où êtes-vous logé ?

How long have you lived here?
Depuis combien de temps habitez-vous ici ?

What's your address, please?
Quelle est votre adresse ?

Are you the owner/tenant?
Vous êtes le propriétaire / locataire ?

Do you like this area?
Vous aimez ce quartier ?

Where are you moving to?
Où déménagez-vous ?

YOU SHOULD KNOW...

Rental agreements can vary according to whether the property is furnished ("meublé") or unfurnished ("vide"). Make sure you understand what your rights are if you intend to rent long-term in France.

country cottage **le gîte rural**	district **le quartier**	rental agreement **le contrat de location**
terraced house **la maison mitoyenne**	owner **le propriétaire / la propriétaire**	holiday let **la location de vacances**
townhouse **la maison de ville**	tenant **le locataire / la locataire**	to rent **louer**
villa **la villa**		to own **posséder**
building **le bâtiment**	neighbour **le voisin / la voisine**	to move house **déménager**
address **l'adresse** *f*	mortgage **le prêt immobilier**	to build a house **construire une maison**
suburb **la banlieue**	rent **le loyer**	

TYPES OF BUILDING

apartment block
l'immeuble *m*

bungalow
le pavillon

detached house
la maison individuelle

farmhouse
la ferme

semi-detached house
la maison jumelée

studio flat
le studio

We are renovating our home.
Nous rénovons la maison.

There's no hot water.
Il n'y a pas d'eau chaude.

We are redecorating the lounge.
Nous refaisons la décoration du salon.

We have a power cut.
Il y a une coupure de courant.

There's a problem with...
Il y a un problème avec...

I need a plumber/an electrician.
J'ai besoin d'un plombier / électricien.

It's not working.
Ça ne marche pas.

Can you recommend anyone?
Connaissez-vous quelqu'un ?

The drains are blocked.
Les canalisations sont bouchées.

Can it be repaired?
C'est réparable ?

The boiler has broken.
La chaudière est en panne.

I can smell gas/smoke.
Ça sent le gaz / la fumée.

What seems to be the problem?
Quel est le problème ?

Where is the meter/fuse box?
Où est le compteur / la boîte à fusibles ?

How long has it been broken/leaking?
C'est cassé / Ça fuit depuis combien de temps ?

Here's a number for a plumber/an electrician.
Voici le numéro d'un plombier / électricien.

room	attic	wall
la pièce	**le grenier**	**le mur**
cellar	ceiling	floor
la cave	**le plafond**	**le sol**

balcony **le balcon**	air conditioning **la climatisation**	skylight **le puits de lumière**
plug/socket **la prise**	central heating **le chauffage central**	dormer **la lucarne**
adaptor **l'adaptateur** m	satellite dish **l'antenne parabolique** f	to fix **réparer**
electricity **l'électricité** f	back door **la porte de derrière**	to decorate **décorer**
plumbing **la plomberie**	French windows **la porte-fenêtre**	to renovate **rénover**

INSIDE

boiler
la chaudière

ceiling fan
le ventilateur de plafond

extension cable
la multiprise

fuse box
la boîte à fusibles

heater
le radiateur

light bulb
l'ampoule f

meter
le compteur

radiator
le radiateur

security alarm
l'alarme *f*

smoke alarm
l'alarme incendie *f*

thermostat
le thermostat

wood-burning stove
le poêle à bois

OUTSIDE

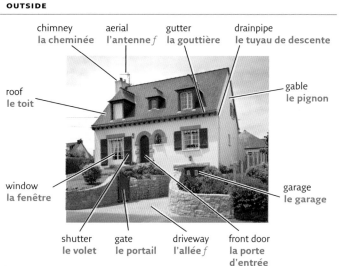

chimney
la cheminée

aerial
l'antenne *f*

gutter
la gouttière

drainpipe
le tuyau de descente

gable
le pignon

roof
le toit

window
la fenêtre

garage
le garage

shutter
le volet

gate
le portail

driveway
l'allée *f*

front door
la porte d'entrée

YOU MIGHT SAY/HEAR...

Would you like to come round?
Voulez-vous passer à la maison ?

Hi! Come in.
Salut ! Entrez.

Make yourself at home.
Faites comme chez vous.

Shall I take my shoes off?
Est-ce que je dois enlever mes chaussures ?

Can I use your bathroom?
Où sont vos toilettes ?

Thanks for inviting me over.
Merci de m'avoir invité.

VOCABULARY

porch/hallway
l'entree *f*

peephole
le judas

doormat
le paillasson

letterbox
la boîte aux lettres

corridor
le couloir

stairwell
la cage d'escalier

staircase
l'escalier *m*

landing
le palier

lift
l'ascenseur *m*

to buzz somebody in
**faire entrer quelqu'un
(par interphone)**

to wipe one's feet
s'essuyer les pieds

to hang one's
jacket up
accrocher sa veste

doorbell
la sonnette

intercom
l'interphone *m*

key
la clé

VOCABULARY

carpet	table lamp	to relax
la moquette	**la lampe de table**	**se détendre**
floorboards	cable/satellite TV	to sit down
le parquet	**la télévision par**	**s'asseoir**
	câble / satellite	
suite		to watch TV
l'ensemble de	smart TV	**regarder la télé**
meubles *m*	**la télévision**	
	intelligente	to listen to music
sofa bed		**écouter de la**
le canapé-lit	TV on demand	**musique**
	la télévision à la	
	demande	

GENERAL

bookcase
la bibliothèque

curtains
les rideaux *mpl*

display cabinet
la vitrine

DVD/Blu-ray® player
le lecteur DVD /
Blu-ray®

radio
la radio

remote control
la télécommande

sideboard
le buffet

TV stand
le meuble télé

Venetian blind
le store vénitien

LOUNGE

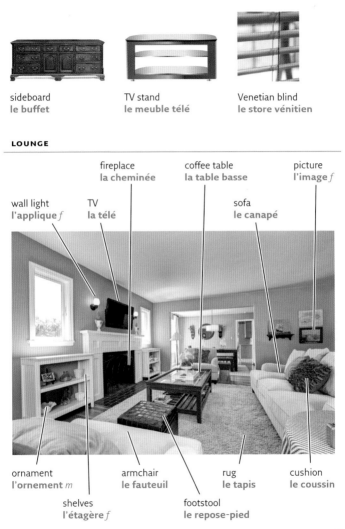

fireplace
la cheminée

coffee table
la table basse

picture
l'image *f*

wall light
l'applique *f*

TV
la télé

sofa
le canapé

ornament
l'ornement *m*

armchair
le fauteuil

rug
le tapis

cushion
le coussin

shelves
l'étagère *f*

footstool
le repose-pied

Kitchens in France are often closed to the rest of the house and aren't usually treated as entertaining spaces. Open-plan kitchens are known in France as "cuisines américaines" (American kitchens).

VOCABULARY

(electric) cooker **la cuisinière**	to cook **cuisiner**	to bake **cuire (au four)**
gas cooker **la gazinière**	to fry **frire**	to wash up **faire la vaisselle**
cooker hood **la hotte**	to stir-fry **faire sauter**	to clean the worktops **débarrasser le plan de travail**
kettle **la bouilloire**	to boil **bouillir**	to put away the groceries **ranger les courses**
toaster **le grille-pain**	to roast **rôtir**	

YOU SHOULD KNOW...

A few typically French kitchen appliances include: raclette iron ("un appareil à raclette") – used to make the Swiss cheese dish raclette; madeleine moulds ("moules à madeleine") – baking tins specially shaped to make madeleines; chinois sieve ("un chinois") – a very fine mesh strainer used for making sauces.

KITCHEN UTENSILS

baking tray
la plaque pour le four

cafetière
la cafetière à piston

casserole dish
la cocotte

chopping board
la planche à découper

colander
la passoire

corkscrew
le tire-bouchon

food processor
le robot de cuisine

frying pan
la poêle

grater
la râpe

hand mixer
le batteur

kitchen knife
le couteau de cuisine

ladle
la louche

masher
le presse-purée

measuring jug
le verre mesureur

mixing bowl
le saladier

peeler
l'économe *m*

rolling pin
le rouleau à pâtisserie

saucepan
la casserole

sieve
le tamis

spatula
la spatule

tin opener
l'ouvre-boîtes *m*

whisk
le fouet

wok
le wok

wooden spoon
la cuillère en bois

MISCELLANEOUS ITEMS

aluminium foil
le papier aluminium

bin bag
le sac poubelle

bread bin
la huche à pain

clingfilm
le film alimentaire

kitchen roll
l'essuie-tout *m*

pedal bin
la poubelle à pédale

KITCHEN

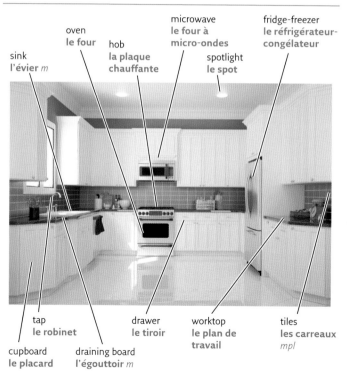

sink
l'évier *m*

oven
le four

hob
la plaque chauffante

microwave
le four à micro-ondes

spotlight
le spot

fridge-freezer
le réfrigérateur-congélateur

tap
le robinet

drawer
le tiroir

worktop
le plan de travail

tiles
les carreaux *mpl*

cupboard
le placard

draining board
l'égouttoir *m*

VOCABULARY

dining table	crockery	to set the table
la table à manger	**la vaisselle**	**mettre la table**
place mat	cutlery	to dine
le set de table	**les couverts** *mpl*	**dîner**
coaster	glassware	to clear the table
le dessous de verre	**la verrerie**	**débarrasser la table**

YOU SHOULD KNOW...

When dining in a French home, it is good table manners to keep your hands on the table. You should not begin eating until the host has wished you "bon appétit" (enjoy your meal).

GENERAL

gravy boat
la saucière

napkin
la serviette

pepper mill
le moulin à poivre

salad bowl
le saladier

salt cellar
la salière

serving dish
le plat de service

bowl
le bol

champagne flute
la flûte à champagne

cup and saucer
la tasse et la soucoupe

knife and fork
le couteau et la fourchette

plate
l'assiette *f*

spoon
la cuillère

teaspoon
la cuillère à café

tumbler
le verre

wine glass
le verre à vin

VOCABULARY

single bed
le lit d'une personne

double bed
le lit deux personnes

master bedroom
la chambre principale

spare room
la chambre d'ami

en-suite bathroom
la salle de bain attenante

nursery
la chambre d'enfant

bedding
la literie

to go to bed
aller se coucher

to sleep
dormir

to wake up
se réveiller

to make the bed
faire le lit

to change the sheets
changer les draps

GENERAL

blanket
la couverture

bunk beds
les lits superposés
mpl

clock radio
le radio-réveil

coat hanger
le portemanteau

dressing table
la coiffeuse

hairdryer
le sèche-cheveux

laundry basket
le panier à linge

quilt
l'édredon *m*

sheets
les draps *mpl*

BEDROOM

chest of drawers
la commode

curtains
les rideaux *mpl*

mirror
le miroir

bed
le lit

wardrobe
l'armoire *f*

duvet
la couette

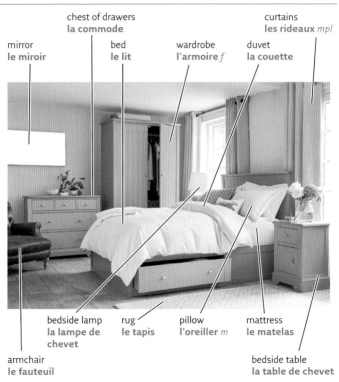

bedside lamp
la lampe de chevet

rug
le tapis

pillow
l'oreiller *m*

mattress
le matelas

armchair
le fauteuil

bedside table
la table de chevet

In many older French homes, toilets may be situated away from the main bathroom. It is also quite common in French homes to see washing machines installed in the bathroom, rather than in the kitchen or utility room.

VOCABULARY

shower curtain **le rideau de douche**	drain **l'égout** *m*	to wash one's hands **se laver les mains**
toilet seat **le siège WC**	to shower **se doucher**	to brush one's teeth **se brosser les dents**
flush **la chasse d'eau**	to have a bath **prendre un bain**	to go to the toilet **aller aux toilettes**

GENERAL

bath mat
le tapis de bain

bath towel
la serviette de bain

face cloth
le gant de toilette

hand towel
l'essuie-mains *m*

shower puff
la fleur de douche

soap
le savon

sponge
l'éponge *f*

toilet brush
la brosse à toilettes

toilet roll
le papier toilette

BATHROOM

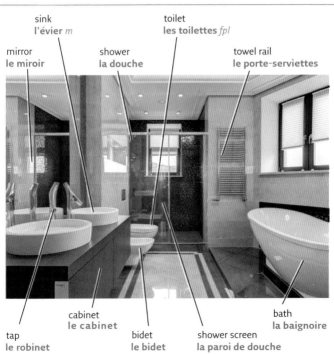

sink
l'évier *m*

toilet
les toilettes *fpl*

mirror
le miroir

shower
la douche

towel rail
le porte-serviettes

cabinet
le cabinet

bath
la baignoire

tap
le robinet

bidet
le bidet

shower screen
la paroi de douche

VOCABULARY

tree
l'arbre *m*

soil
la terre

grass
l'herbe *f*

plant
la plante

weed
la mauvaise herbe

flowerbed
la plate-bande

compost
le compost

allotment
le jardin ouvrier

gardener
**le jardinier /
la jardinière**

to weed
désherber

to water
arroser

to grow
cultiver

to plant
planter

GENERAL

decking
la terrasse en bois

garden fork
la fourche

garden hose
le tuyau

gardening gloves
**les gants de
jardinage** *mpl*

garden shed
la cabane

greenhouse
la serre

hoe
la binette

lawnmower
la tondeuse

parasol
le parasol

plant pot
le pot de fleurs

pruners
le sécateur

spade
la pelle

trowel
le déplantoir

watering can
l'arrosoir *m*

weedkiller
le désherbant

Wellington boots
les bottes en caoutchouc *fpl*

wheelbarrow
la brouette

window box
la jardinière

lawn
la pelouse

shrub
l'arbuste *m*

gate
le portail

fence
la palissade

trellis
le treillis

bird box
le nichoir

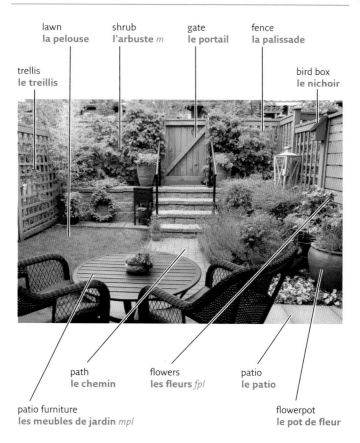

path
le chemin

flowers
les fleurs *fpl*

patio
le patio

patio furniture
les meubles de jardin *mpl*

flowerpot
le pot de fleur

VOCABULARY

utility room
la buanderie

household appliances
**les appareils
électroménagers** *mpl*

chores
**les tâches
ménagères** *fpl*

basin
la bassine

bleach
l'eau de javel *f*

disinfectant
le désinfectant

dishwasher tablet
**la pastille
lave-vaisselle**

laundry detergent
la lessive

recycling bin
**la poubelle de
recyclage**

wastepaper basket
la corbeille

washing-up liquid
le liquide vaisselle

to sweep the floor
balayer le sol

to do the laundry
faire la lessive

to hoover
passer l'aspirateur

to tidy up
ranger

to clean
nettoyer

to take out the bin
sortir les poubelles

brush
la brosse

bucket
le seau

cloth
le torchon

clothes horse
l'étendoir *m*

clothes pegs
les pinces à linge *fpl*

dishwasher
le lave-vaisselle

dustbin
la poubelle

dustpan
la pelle

iron
le fer à repasser

ironing board
la planche à repasser

mop
la serpillière

rubber gloves
les gants en caoutchouc *mpl*

scourer
le tampon à récurer

tea towel
le torchon (à vaisselle)

tumble drier
le sèche-linge

vacuum cleaner
l'aspirateur *m*

washing line
la corde à linge

washing machine
la machine à laver

AT THE SHOPS | AUX MAGASINS

Markets full of lush produce and local specialities, the smell of freshly baked bread from the boulangerie, or chic boutiques selling French fashions – just some of the things that might spring to mind when it comes to shopping in France. That's not to say that you won't find plenty of large supermarkets, busy shopping centres, and many familiar international chains in urban areas.

basket
le panier

banana
la banane

bread
le pain

vegetable oil
**l'huile
végétale** *f*

Most stores in France are open from Monday to Saturday; however, in some towns and villages it is common for local shops to have reduced opening hours on Mondays. Many shops will also shut between 12 p.m. and 2 p.m. for lunch throughout the week. It is rare to find 24-hour shops and supermarkets, even in the biggest cities in France.

YOU MIGHT SAY...

Where is the...?
Où est le / la...?

Where is the nearest...?
Où est le / la ... le / la plus proche ?

Where can I buy...?
Où est-ce qu'on peut acheter...?

What time do you open/close?
Vous ouvrez / fermez à quelle heure ?

I'm just looking.
Je ne fais que regarder, merci.

Do you sell...?
Est-ce que vous avez...?

May I have...?
Je vais prendre...

Can I pay by cash/card?
Est-ce que je peux payer en liquide / par carte ?

Can I pay with my mobile app?
Est-ce que je peux payer avec mon smartphone ?

How much does this cost?
Ça coûte combien ?

How much is delivery?
Combien coûte la livraison ?

I need...
J'aurais besoin de...

I would like...
Je voudrais...

Can I exchange this?
C'est possible d'échanger cet article ?

Can I get a refund?
Est-ce que je peux me faire rembourser ?

That's all, thank you.
C'est tout, merci.

YOU SHOULD KNOW...

Distribution of single-use plastic bags is banned in French shops – many stores have introduced paper bags and reusable plastic bags that can be purchased.

mayonnaise
la mayonnaise

noodles
les nouilles *fpl*

olive oil
l'huile d'olive *f*

pasta
les pâtes *fpl*

pepper
le poivre

rice
le riz

salt
le sel

spices
les épices *fpl*

sugar
le sucre

teabags
les sachets de thé
mpl

vegetable oil
l'huile végétale *f*

vinegar
le vinaigre

chocolate
le chocolat

crisps
les chips *fpl*

nuts
les fruits à coque *mpl*

olives
les olives *mpl*

popcorn
le popcorn

sweets
les bonbons *mpl*

DRINKS

beer
la bière

fizzy drink
la boisson gazeuse

fruit juice
le jus de fruit

mineral water
l'eau minérale *f*

spirits
les spiritueux *mpl*

wine
le vin

Most markets will be set up early in the morning and will wind down by lunchtime. It's worth getting up early to buy the freshest produce on offer.

YOU MIGHT SAY...

Where is the market?
Où est le marché ?

When is market day?
Le marché a lieu quel jour ?

A kilo/100 grams of...
Un kilo / Cent grammes de...

Two/Three ..., please.
Deux / Trois ..., s'il vous plaît.

What do I owe you?
Combien je vous dois ?

YOU MIGHT HEAR...

The market is in the square.
Le marché se trouve sur la place.

The market is on a Tuesday.
Le marché a lieu le mardi.

Can I help you?
Je peux vous aider ?

Here you go. Anything else?
Voilà. Et avec ceci ?

Here's your change.
Voici votre monnaie.

VOCABULARY

marketplace
la place du marché

traditional production
la fabrication artisanale

flea market
le marché aux puces

indoor market
le marché couvert

farmer's market
le marché fermier

trader
le commerçant / la commerçante

stall
l'étal *m*

produce
les produits *mpl*

local
local

organic
bio

seasonal
saisonnier

home-made
fait maison

YOU SHOULD KNOW...

Haggling would not be expected at the stalls of a fruit and vegetable market; it's a different story at the flea market!

YOU MIGHT SAY...

Do you have...?
Est-ce que vous avez...?

Are they ripe/fresh?
Est-ce qu'ils sont mûrs / frais ?

YOU MIGHT HEAR...

What would you like?
Qu'est-ce que vous désirez ?

They are very fresh.
Ils sont tout frais.

VOCABULARY

grocer's **l'épicerie** f	segment **le quartier**	unripe **pas mûr**
juice **le jus**	skin **la peau**	seedless **sans pépins**
leaf **la feuille**	stone **le noyau**	to chop **couper**
peel **la pelure**	raw **cru**	to dice **couper en dés**
pip **le pépin**	fresh **frais**	to grate **râper**
rind **le zeste**	rotten **pourri**	to juice **faire du jus de**
seed **la graine**	ripe **mûr**	to peel **peler**

YOU SHOULD KNOW...

Remember that when buying fruit or vegetables from the supermarket, customers are usually required to weigh and sticker their purchases before going to the checkouts.

apple
la pomme

apricot
l'abricot *m*

banana
la banane

blackberry
la mûre

blackcurrant
le cassis

blueberry
la myrtille

cherry
la cerise

gooseberry
la groseille à maquereau

grape
le raisin

grapefruit
le pamplemousse

kiwi fruit
le kiwi

lemon
le citron

mango
la mangue

melon
le melon

orange
l'orange *f*

passion fruit
le fruit de la passion

peach
la pêche

pear
la poire

pineapple
l'ananas *m*

plum
la prune

raspberry
la framboise

redcurrant
la groseille

strawberry
la fraise

watermelon
la pastèque

artichoke
l'artichaut *m*

asparagus
l'asperge *f*

aubergine
l'aubergine *f*

beetroot
la betterave

broccoli
les brocolis *mpl*

Brussels sprout
le chou de Bruxelles

cabbage
le chou

carrot
la carotte

cauliflower
le chou-fleur

celery
le céleri

chilli
le piment

courgette
la courgette

cucumber
le concombre

garlic
l'ail *m*

green beans
les haricots verts *mpl*

leek
le poireau

lettuce
la laitue

mushroom
le champignon

onion
l'oignon *m*

peas
les petits pois *mpl*

potato
la pomme de terre

red pepper
le poivron rouge

spinach
les épinards *mpl*

tomato
la tomate

Ask the fishmonger for tips on what is fresh, what has been frozen, and what is in season.

YOU MIGHT SAY...

How fresh is this fish?
Quand est-ce que ce poisson a été pêché ?

I'd like this filleted, please.
Je voudrais que vous leviez les filets, s'il vous plaît.

Can you remove the bones?
Est-ce que vous pouvez enlever les arêtes ?

YOU MIGHT HEAR...

This fish was landed...
Ce poisson a été pris...

Would you like to have this filleted?
Est-ce que vous voulez qu'on lève les filets ?

VOCABULARY

fishmonger
le poissonnier /
la poissonnière

(fish)bone
l'arête f

fillet
le filet

roe
les œufs de poisson mpl

scales
les écailles fpl

shellfish
les crustacés mpl

shell
la coquille

freshwater
d'eau douce

saltwater
de mer

farmed
d'élevage

wild
sauvage

salted
salé

smoked
fumé

filleted
découpé en filets

deboned
désarêté

YOU SHOULD KNOW...

Fishmongers will also sell snails ("escargots") and, less commonly, frogs' legs ("cuisses de grenouille").

cod
le cabillaud

haddock
l'aiglefin *m*

herring
le hareng

lemon sole
la limande-sole

mackerel
le maquereau

salmon
le saumon

sardine
la sardine

sea bass
le bar

sea bream
la dorade

skate
la raie

trout
la truite

tuna
le thon

clam
la palourde

crab
le crabe

crayfish
l'écrevisse *f*

lobster
le homard

mussel
la moule

octopus
la pieuvre

oyster
l'huître *f*

prawn
la crevette

scallop
**la coquille
Saint-Jacques**

sea urchin
l'oursin *m*

shrimp
la crevette

squid
le calamar

Butchers in France are often able to recommend what kind of cuts of meat to buy for the recipes you'd like to try, as well as local specialities they may sell.

YOU MIGHT SAY...

A kilo of...
Un kilo de...

A slice of ..., please.
Une tranche de ..., s'il vous plaît.

Can you slice this for me, please?
Est-ce que vous pouvez me le trancher, s'il vous plaît ?

What is the best cut for...?
Quel est le meilleur morceau pour...?

YOU MIGHT HEAR...

Certainly, sir/madam.
Oui monsieur / madame.

How much would you like?
Vous en voulez quelle quantité ?

How many would you like?
Vous en voulez combien ?

I'd recommend...
Je vous conseillerais...

VOCABULARY

butcher le boucher / la bouchère	beef le bœuf	duck le canard
meat la viande	pork le porc	goose l'oie *f*
red meat la viande rouge	lamb l'agneau *m*	turkey la dinde
white meat la viande blanche	game le gibier	offal les abats *mpl*
charcuterie la charcuterie	venison la venaison	cooked cuit
cut (of meat) le morceau (de viande)	veal le veau	raw cru
pâté le pâté	poultry la volaille	free-range élevé en plein air

bacon
le bacon

burger
le steak haché

chicken breast
le blanc de poulet

chop
la côtelette

(cured) sausage
le saucisson

ham
le jambon

joint
le rôti

lardons
les lardons *mpl*

mince
la viande hachée

ribs
les côtes *fpl*

sausages
les saucisses *fpl*

steak
le steak

There are strict regulations in place to define what is and isn't a boulangerie in France. Boulangeries must make their bread on-site without preservatives or additives, and cannot freeze the dough or baguettes that they produce for sale.

YOU MIGHT SAY...

Do you sell...?
Est-ce que vous avez...?

Could I have...?
Je vais prendre...

How much are...?
À combien sont les...?

YOU MIGHT HEAR...

Are you being served?
Est-ce qu'on s'occupe de vous ?

Would you like anything else?
Et avec ceci ?

It costs...
Ça fait...

VOCABULARY

baker
le boulanger /
la boulangère

bread
le pain

loaf
un pain

slice
une tranche

crust
la croûte

dough
la pâte

flour
la farine

gluten-free
sans gluten

to bake
faire cuire au four

YOU SHOULD KNOW...

A "dépôt de pain" is a shop or counter that sells bakery products that have been baked off-site.

almond croissant
le croissant aux
amandes

baguette
la baguette

bread rolls
les petits pains *mpl*

brioche
la brioche

croissant
le croissant

Danish pastry
le feuilleté

doughnut
le beignet

éclair
l'éclair *m*

fruit tart
la tarte aux fruits

macaroon
le macaron

mille-feuille
le millefeuille

pain au chocolat
le pain au chocolat

pancakes
les crêpes *mpl*

waffle
la gaufre

wholemeal bread
le pain complet

Cheese is a hugely important part of the French diet. Cheesemongers are usually happy to give their recommendations and may allow you to taste samples.

VOCABULARY

cheese	blue cheese	cream cheese
le fromage	le bleu	le fromage à tartiner

YOU SHOULD KNOW...

"AOC" stands for "appellation d'origine contrôlée", which indicates that a product comes from a specific region or area. It is perceived as a guarantee of quality and speciality. Over 40 French cheeses and 300 French wines carry an AOC label.

brie	Camembert	Cantal
le brie	le camembert	le cantal
cheddar	Comté	cottage cheese
le cheddar	le comté	le fromage blanc maigre

Emmenthal
l'emmental *m*

Époisses
l'époisses *f*

goat's cheese
le fromage de chèvre

Manchego
le manchego

mozzarella
la mozzarella

parmesan
le parmesan

Roquefort
le roquefort

reblochon
le reblochon

Stilton®
le stilton

UHT milk is much more widely used in France than in the UK, but it is also possible to find fresh milk in the supermarkets, or buy unpasteurized "lait cru" directly from dairy farmers.

VOCABULARY

egg white
le blanc d'œuf

egg yolk
le jaune d'œuf

whole milk
le lait entier

skimmed/semi-skimmed milk
le lait écrémé / demi-écrémé

UHT milk
le lait UHT

soymilk
le lait de soja

single/double cream
la crème liquide / épaisse

sour cream
la crème aigre

free-range
de poules élevées en plein air

pasteurized
pasteurisé

unpasteurized
non pasteurisé

dairy-free
sans produits laitiers

butter
le beurre

cream
la crème

egg
l'œuf *m*

margarine
la margarine

milk
le lait

yoghurt
le yaourt

PHARMACY | LA PHARMACIE

In France, pharmacies are owned and run by individual pharmacists, so you don't see pharmacy chains in French towns and villages. Many pharmacies also have "parapharmacies", where you can buy non-pharmaceuticals, cosmetics, and hygiene products. You cannot buy medicines from a "parapharmacie".

YOU MIGHT SAY...

I need something for...
Est-ce que vous avez quelque chose pour...?

I'm allergic to...
Je suis allergique à...

I'm collecting a prescription.
Je viens chercher mes médicaments.

What would you recommend?
Qu'est-ce que vous conseillez ?

Is this suitable for young children?
Est-ce que ça convient pour les enfants en bas âge ?

YOU MIGHT HEAR...

Do you have a prescription?
Vous avez une ordonnance ?

Do you have ID?
Vous avez une pièce d'identité ?

Do you have any allergies?
Est-ce que vous avez des allergies ?

Take two tablets twice a day.
Prenez deux cachets deux fois par jour.

You should see a doctor.
Vous devriez voir un médecin.

I'd recommend...
Je vous conseillerais...

VOCABULARY

pharmacist
le pharmacien / la pharmacienne

prescription
l'ordonnance f

antihistamine
l'antihistaminique m

decongestant
le décongestif

painkiller
l'analgésique m

handwash
le savon liquide mains

fragrance
le parfum

cold
le rhume

diarrhoea
la diarrhée

hay fever
le rhume des foins

headache/ stomachache
le mal de tête / ventre

sore throat
le mal de gorge

93

antiseptic cream
la crème antiseptique

bandage
le bandage

capsule
la capsule

condom
le préservatif

cough mixture
le sirop pour la toux

drops
les gouttes *fpl*

insect repellent
le répulsif à insectes

lozenge
la pastille

medicine
le médicament

plaster
le pansement

suntan lotion
la crème solaire

tablet/pill
le cachet

antiperspirant
l'antitranspirant *m*

conditioner
l'après-shampooing
m

mouthwash
le bain de bouche

razor
le rasoir

sanitary towel
**la serviette
hygiénique**

shampoo
le shampooing

shaving foam
la mousse à raser

shower gel
le gel douche

soap
le savon

tampon
le tampon

toothbrush
la brosse à dents

toothpaste
le dentifrice

blusher
le fard à joues

comb
le peigne

eyeliner
l'eye-liner *m*

eyeshadow
le fard à paupières

foundation
le fond de teint

hairbrush
la brosse à cheveux

hairspray
la laque

lip balm
le baume à lèvres

lipstick
le rouge à lèvres

mascara
le mascara

nail varnish
le vernis à ongles

powder
la poudre

If you intend to travel to France with your baby, it may be possible to hire the equipment you require from specialist companies.

VOCABULARY

colic **les coliques** *fpl*	nappy sack **le sac hygiénique**	to breast-feed **allaiter**
disposable/reusable nappy **la couche jetable / lavable**	nappy rash **l'érythème fessier** *m*	to be teething **faire ses dents**
	teething gel **le gel de dentition**	

CLOTHING

Babygro®/sleepsuit
la grenouillère

bib
le bavoir

bootees
les chaussons de bébé *mpl*

mittens
les moufles *fpl*

snowsuit
la combinaison rembourrée

vest
le body

baby food
**les aliments pour
bébés** *mpl*

baby lotion
**la crème hydratante
pour bébé**

baby's bottle
le biberon

changing bag
le sac à langer

cotton bud
le coton-tige

cotton wool
le coton hydrophile

formula milk
le lait maternisé

nappy
la couche

nappy cream
**la crème pour
le change**

rusk
la biscotte

talcum powder
le talc

wet wipes
**les lingettes
humides** *fpl*

baby bath
la baignoire pour bébé

baby seat
le siège bébé

baby walker
le trotteur

cot
le lit d'enfant

dummy
la tétine

highchair
la chaise haute

mobile
le mobile

Moses basket
le couffin

pram
le landau

pushchair
la poussette

teething ring
l'anneau de dentition *m*

travel cot
le lit-parapluie

As well as newspapers and magazines, French newsagents may also sell tobacco, stamps, and tickets for local public transport.

VOCABULARY

kiosk
le kiosque

tobacconist
le (bureau de) tabac

vendor
**le vendeur /
la vendeuse**

broadsheet
**le journal grand
format**

tabloid
le tabloïd

book of tickets
le carnet

stationery
**les fournitures de
bureau** *fpl*

daily
quotidien

weekly
hebdomadaire

GENERAL

book
le livre

cigar
le cigare

cigarette
la cigarette

comic book
la bande dessinée

confectionery
la confiserie

e-cigarette
**la cigarette
électronique**

envelope
l'enveloppe *f*

greetings card
la carte de vœux

magazine
le magazine

map
la carte

newspaper
le journal

notebook
le carnet

pen
le stylo

pencil
le crayon

postcard
la carte postale

puzzle book
**le livre de
casse-têtes**

scratch card
la carte à gratter

stamp
le timbre

The department store is a firm fixture of the Parisian shopping scene, and there are plenty to visit in the capital. Note that while many smaller stores will close at midday for lunch, many department stores will remain open for the whole afternoon – a practice known as "la journée continue" in France.

YOU MIGHT SAY...

Where is the menswear department?
Où est le rayon hommes ?

Which floor is this?
On est à quel étage ?

Can you gift-wrap this, please?
Est-ce que vous pouvez faire un paquet-cadeau ?

Are there any toilets in the store?
Est-ce qu'il y a des toilettes dans ce magasin ?

YOU MIGHT HEAR...

Menswear is on the second floor.
Le rayon hommes est au deuxième étage.

This is the first floor.
On est au premier étage.

Would you like this gift-wrapped?
Est-ce que vous voulez un paquet-cadeau ?

The lift is over there.
L'ascenseur est par là.

VOCABULARY

brand
la marque

counter
le comptoir

department
le rayon

floor
l'étage *m*

escalator
l'escalator *m*

lift
l'ascenseur *m*

toilets
les toilettes *fpl*

sale
les soldes *mpl*

womenswear
les vêtements pour femmes *mpl*

menswear
les vêtements pour hommes *mpl*

sportswear
les vêtements de sport *mpl*

swimwear
les maillots de bain *mpl*

accessories
les accessoires de mode *mpl*

cosmetics
les produits de beauté *mpl*

fashion
la mode

food and drink
l'alimentation *f*

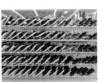

footwear
les chaussures *fpl*

furniture
les meubles *mpl*

kitchenware
les ustensiles de cuisine *mpl*

leather goods
la maroquinerie

lighting
l'éclairage *m*

lingerie
la lingerie

soft furnishings
les tissus d'ameublement *mpl*

toys
les jouets *mpl*

France is famous for fashion and the Champs-Elysées is maybe the most famous shopping street in the world. This area of Paris is home to some of the world's most famous fashion houses, as well as more affordable French brands. The area is known simply as "les Champs" by many Parisians.

YOU MIGHT SAY...

I'm just looking, thank you.
Je ne fais que regarder, merci.

I'd like to try this on, please.
Je voudrais l'essayer, s'il vous plaît.

Where are the fitting rooms?
Où sont les cabines d'essayage ?

I'm a size...
Je fais du...

Have you got a bigger/smaller size? (clothing)
Vous avez la taille au-dessus / au-dessous ?

Have you got a bigger/smaller size? (shoes)
Vous avez la pointure au-dessus / au-dessous ?

This is too small/big.
C'est trop petit / grand.

This is too tight/short/long.
C'est trop serré / court / long.

This is torn.
C'est déchiré.

It's not my style.
La coupe ne me va pas.

YOU MIGHT HEAR...

Can I help you?
Je peux vous aider ?

Let me know if I can help.
N'hésitez pas si vous avez besoin d'un renseignement.

The fitting rooms are over there.
Les cabines sont par là.

What size are you? (clothing)
Quelle taille faites-vous ?

What size are you? (shoes)
Quelle pointure faites-vous ?

I'm sorry, it's out of stock.
Je suis désolé, ce modèle est indisponible.

I'm sorry, we don't have that size/colour.
Je suis désolé, nous n'avons pas cette taille / couleur.

I can get you another one.
Je vous en apporte un autre.

That suits you.
Ça vous va bien.

clothes/clothing **les vêtements** *mpl*	umbrella **le parapluie**	cotton **le coton**
shoes/footwear **les chaussures** *fpl*	size (clothing) **la taille**	leather **le cuir**
underwear **les sous-vêtements** *mpl*	size (shoe) **la pointure**	silk **la soie**
	casual **décontracté**	petite **petite taille**
fitting room **la cabine d'essayage**	smart **élégant**	plus-size **grande taille**
wallet **le portefeuille**	wool **la laine**	to try on **essayer**
purse **le porte-monnaie**	denim **le jean**	to fit **être à la bonne taille**
jewellery **les bijoux** *mpl*		

CLOTHING

bikini
le bikini

blouse
le chemisier

boxer shorts
le caleçon

bra
le soutien-gorge

cardigan
le gilet

coat
le manteau

dress
la robe

dressing gown
la robe de chambre

jacket
la veste

jeans
le jean

jogging bottoms
le pantalon de survêtement

jumper
le pull

leggings
les leggings *mpl*

pants
le slip

pyjamas
le pyjama

shirt
la chemise

shorts
le short

skirt
la jupe

socks
les chaussettes *fpl*

sweatshirt
le sweat

swimsuit
le maillot de bain

(three-piece) suit
le costume

tie
la cravate

tights
les collants *mpl*

trousers
le pantalon

T-shirt
le t-shirt

waterproof jacket
l'imperméable *m*

ACCESSORIES

baseball cap
la casquette

belt
la ceinture

bracelet
le bracelet

earrings
les boucles d'oreille
fpl

gloves
les gants *mpl*

handbag
le sac à main

necklace
le collier

scarf
le foulard

woolly hat
le bonnet

FOOTWEAR

boots
les bottes *fpl*

high heels
les talons hauts *mpl*

lace-up shoes
les chaussures à lacets *fpl*

sandals
les sandales *fpl*

slippers
les pantoufles *fpl*

trainers
les baskets *fpl*

From local retail and trade merchants to numerous larger chain stores, there are many options available for anybody who is looking for some DIY essentials.

VOCABULARY

home improvements
le bricolage

toolbox
la boîte à outils

interior decorating
la décoration

hardware shop
la quincaillerie

electricity
l'électricité *f*

plumbing
la plomberie

tool
l'outil *m*

joinery
la menuiserie

to do DIY
faire du bricolage

power tool
l'outil électrique *m*

painting
la peinture

to decorate
décorer

chisel
le burin

electric drill
la perceuse électrique

hammer
le marteau

nails
les clous *mpl*

nuts and bolts
les écrous et boulons *mpl*

paint
la peinture

paintbrush
le pinceau

paint roller
le rouleau à peinture

pliers
la tenaille

saw
la scie

screwdriver
le tournevis

screws
les vis *fpl*

spanner
la clé

spirit level
le niveau à bulle

stepladder
l'escabeau *m*

tiles
les carreaux *mpl*

wallpaper
le papier peint

wrench
la clé à molette

In France, breakfast tends to be a smaller, lighter meal than it is in other countries. Most French people will eat breakfast at home as opposed to on the go.

VOCABULARY

breakfast bar **le bar de cuisine**	bread and jam **la tartine de confiture**	to have breakfast **prendre le petit-déjeuner**
bread and butter **la tartine de beurre**	to spread **tartiner**	to skip breakfast **sauter le petit-déjeuner**

YOU SHOULD KNOW...

The word "chocolatine" is often used in the South of France as another name for "pain au chocolat".

DRINKS

coffee
le café

coffee with milk
le café au lait

hot chocolate
le chocolat chaud

milk
le lait

orange juice
le jus d'orange

tea
le thé

baguette
la baguette

bread rolls
les petits pains *mpl*

cereal
les céréales *fpl*

chocolate spread
la pâte à tartiner

croissant
le croissant

jam
la confiture

pain au chocolat
le pain au chocolat

muesli
le muesli

tartine
la tartine

Lunch is often seen as the most important meal of the day in France and it can often involve two or three courses. Many businesses will close for an hour or two for lunch.

YOU MIGHT SAY...

What's for dinner?
Qu'est-ce qu'on mange ce soir ?

What time is lunch?
On mange à quelle heure ce midi ?

May I have...?
Est-ce que je peux avoir...?

Can I try it?
Je peux goûter ?

I can't eat...
Je ne peux pas manger...

YOU MIGHT HEAR...

We're having ... for dinner.
On mange ... ce soir.

Lunch is at midday.
Le déjeuner est à midi.

Dinner's ready!
À table !

Would you like...?
Voulez-vous...?

Is there anything you can't eat?
Y a-t-il des choses que vous ne pouvez pas manger ?

VOCABULARY

food **la nourriture**	courses **les plats** *mpl*	to have lunch **déjeuner**
drink **la boisson**	recipe **la recette**	to have dinner **dîner**
lunch **le déjeuner**	aperitif **l'apéritif** *m*	to eat out **aller au restaurant**
dinner **le dîner**	digestif **le digestif**	

YOU SHOULD KNOW...

The French don't tend to snack between meals, but children will often have an after-school snack, a custom known as "le goûter" or "quatre-heures".

baked eggs
les œufs en cocotte
mpl

broth
le bouillon

cold meats
les viandes froides
fpl

Nicoise salad
la salade niçoise

pâté
le pâté

savoury tart
la quiche

smoked salmon
le saumon fumé

soup
la soupe

soufflé
le soufflé

chips
les frites *fpl*

cooked vegetables
les légumes cuits
mpl

couscous
le couscous

gratin
le gratin

green salad
la salade verte

mixed salad
la salade composée

noodles
les nouilles *fpl*

olives
les olives *mpl*

pasta
les pâtes *fpl*

potatoes
les pommes de terre
fpl

raw vegetables
les crudités *fpl*

rice
le riz

beef bourguignon
le bœuf bourguignon

cassoulet
le cassoulet

coq au vin
le coq au vin

duck confit
le confit de canard

fish soup
la bouillabaisse

French onion soup
la soupe à l'oignon

mussels in white wine
les moules marinières *fpl*

poached skate
la raie meunière

quiche lorraine
la quiche lorraine

ratatouille
la ratatouille

snails in garlic butter
les escargots à la bourguignonne *mpl*

tarte flambée
la tarte flambée

apple tart
la tarte aux pommes

chocolate cake
le gâteau au chocolat

chocolate mousse
la mousse au chocolat

crème brûlée
la crème brûlée

flan
le flan

fruit tart
la tarte aux fruits

ice cream
la glace

lemon tart
la tarte au citron

meringue
la meringue

profiteroles
les profiteroles *fpl*

rum baba
le baba au rhum

sorbet
le sorbet

France is renowned the world over for its cuisine, so it goes without saying that eating out is an important social experience in French culture.

YOU MIGHT SAY...

I'd like to make a reservation.
J'aimerais réserver.

A table for four, please.
Une table pour quatre, s'il vous plaît.

We're ready to order.
Nous sommes prêts à commander.

What would you recommend?
Qu'est-ce que vous conseillez ?

What are the specials today?
Quels sont les plats du jour ?

May I have ..., please?
Je peux avoir ..., s'il vous plaît ?

Are there vegetarian/vegan options?
Y a-t-il un menu végétarien / végétalien ?

I'm allergic to...
Je suis allergique à...

Excuse me, this is cold.
Excusez-moi, c'est froid.

This is not what I ordered.
Ce n'est pas ce que j'ai commandé.

May we have the bill, please?
L'addition, s'il vous plaît.

YOU MIGHT HEAR...

At what time?
À quelle heure ?

How many people?
Combien de personnes ?

Sorry, we're fully booked.
Désolé, nous sommes complets.

Would you like anything to drink?
Désirez-vous des boissons ?

Are you ready to order?
Êtes-vous prêts à commander ?

I would recommend...
Je vous conseille...

The specials today are...
Les plats du jour sont...

I will let the chef know.
Je vais en parler au chef.

Enjoy your meal!
Bon appétit !

122

set menu **le menu**	wine waiter **le sommelier / la sommelière**	dairy-free **sans produits laitiers**
daily specials **les plats du jour** *mpl*	vegetarian **végétarien**	to order **commander**
service charge **le service**	vegan **végétalien**	to ask for the bill **demander l'addition**
tip **le pourboire**	gluten-free **sans gluten**	to be served **être servi**

YOU SHOULD KNOW...

Bread is usually provided for free in French restaurants. However, it's bad etiquette to start eating it before your meal arrives. You don't usually get butter to use as a spread – rather, use the bread to mop up the sauce from your meal.

bar
le bar

bill
la note

bread basket
la corbeille à pain

chair
la chaise

champagne flute
la flûte à champagne

cheese knife
le couteau à fromage

fish knife
le couteau à poisson

jug of water
la carafe d'eau

menu
la carte

napkin
la serviette

salt and pepper
du sel et du poivre

steak knife
le couteau à viande

table
la table

tablecloth
la nappe

toothpicks
les cure-dents *mpl*

vinegar and oil
du vinaigre et de l'huile

waiter/waitress
**le serveur /
la serveuse**

wine glass
le verre à vin

Fast food may not be the first thing you think of when it comes to French dining, but there are still plenty of options for eating on the go.

YOU MIGHT SAY...

I'd like to order, please.
J'aimerais commander, s'il vous plaît.

Do you deliver?
Vous faites les livraisons ?

I'm sitting in/taking away.
Sur place. / À emporter.

How long will it be?
Combien de temps cela va-t-il prendre ?

That's everything, thanks.
Ce sera tout, merci.

YOU MIGHT HEAR...

Can I help you?
Je peux vous aider ?

Sit-in or takeaway?
Sur place ou à emporter ?

We do/don't do delivery.
Nous faisons / ne faisons pas de livraison.

Would you like anything else?
Et avec ceci ?

Small, medium, or large?
Petit, moyen ou grand ?

VOCABULARY

fast-food chain
la chaîne de fast-food

food stall
le stand de nourriture

street food
la cuisine de rue

vendor
le vendeur / la vendeuse

drive-thru
le drive-in

an order to go/ a takeaway
un plat à emporter

delivery charge
les frais de livraison *mpl*

delivery man/woman
le livreur / la livreuse

to phone in an order
passer commande par téléphone

to place an order
passer commande

to collect an order
récupérer des plats

burger
le hamburger

filled baguette
le sandwich

fries
les frites *fpl*

hot dog
le hot dog

kebab
la brochette

omelette
l'omelette *f*

pancakes
les crêpes *mpl*

pizza
la pizza

sandwich
le sandwich

sushi
le sushi

toasted ham and
cheese sandwich
le croque-monsieur

wrap
le wrap

Technology plays a huge role in people's everyday lives. A mere click, tap, or swipe helps us to stay in touch with friends and family, keep up to date with what's going on, and find the information we need.

YOU MIGHT SAY/HEAR...

I'll give you a call later.
Je vous appellerai plus tard.

I'll text/email you.
Je vous enverrai un SMS / e-mail.

What's your number?
Quel est votre numéro de téléphone ?

This is a bad line.
La qualité de l'appel est mauvaise.

I don't have any signal/WiFi.
Je n'ai pas de réseau / wifi.

What's your email address?
Quelle est votre adresse e-mail ?

The website address is...
L'adresse du site est...

What's the WiFi password?
Quel est le mot de passe pour le wifi ?

It's all one word.
C'est en un seul mot.

It's upper/lower case.
C'est en majuscules / minuscules.

VOCABULARY

post **le post**	internet **l'internet** m	mouse **la souris**
social media **les réseaux sociaux** mpl	WiFi **le wifi**	mouse mat **le tapis de souris**
email **l'e-mail** m	website **le site web**	keyboard **le clavier**
email address **l'adresse électronique** f	link **le lien**	app **l'appli** f
	icon **l'icône** f	

data **les données mobiles** *fpl*	voice mail **le message vocal**	to make a phone call **passer un appel**
mobile phone **le téléphone portable**	touchscreen **l'écran tactile** *m*	to post (online) **poster (en ligne)**
landline **la ligne fixe**	screen **l'écran** *m*	to download/upload **télécharger**
text message **le SMS**	button **le bouton**	to charge your phone **charger son portable**
phone signal **le signal de téléphonie mobile**	battery **la batterie**	to switch on/off **allumer / éteindre**
	cable **le câble**	to click on **cliquer sur**

YOU SHOULD KNOW...

Computer keyboards in France use the AZERTY layout, rather than the QWERTY one we are used to in the UK.

charger
le chargeur

computer
l'ordinateur *m*

SIM card
la carte SIM

smartphone
le smartphone

tablet
la tablette

wireless router
le routeur sans fil

Compulsory education in France begins at age 6 through to age 16. Nursery schooling is optional, but parents can apply to the local "mairie" (town hall) to register their child in a state nursery that is provided free of charge.

YOU MIGHT SAY...

What are you studying?
Qu'est-ce que tu étudies ?

What year are you in?
En quelle année es-tu ?

What's your favourite subject?
Quelle est ta matière préférée ?

Do you have any homework?
As-tu des devoirs ?

YOU MIGHT HEAR...

I'm studying...
Je fais des études de...

I'm in Year 6/my final year.
Je suis en sixième année / en dernière année.

I enjoy...
J'aime bien...

I have an assignment.
J'ai un devoir.

VOCABULARY

nursery school
l'école maternelle f

primary school
l'école primaire f

middle school
le collège

high school
le lycée

higher education
l'enseignement supérieur m

university
l'université f

pupil
l'élève m / **l'élève** f

teacher
le professeur / la professeure

headteacher
le principal / la principale

classroom
la salle de classe

janitor
le concierge / la concierge

timetable
l'emploi du temps m

lesson
la leçon

lecture
le cours

tutorial
le didacticiel

homework
les devoirs mpl

exam
l'examen m

degree
le diplôme (universitaire)

undergraduate
l'étudiant en premier cycle *m* /
l'étudiante en premier cycle *f*

postgraduate
l'étudiant en troisième cycle *m* /
l'étudiante en troisième cycle *f*

canteen
la cantine

playing field
le terrain de jeu

halls of residence
la résidence universitaire

student union
le foyer des étudiants

student card
la carte d'étudiant

to learn
apprendre

to teach
enseigner

to revise
réviser

to sit an exam
passer un examen

to graduate
obtenir son diplôme

to study
étudier

SCHOOL

colouring pencils
les crayons de couleur *mpl*

eraser
la gomme

exercise book
le cahier de cours

paper
le papier

pen
le stylo

pencil
le crayon

pencil case
la trousse

ruler
la règle

schoolbag
le cartable

sharpener
le taille-crayon

textbook
le manuel

whiteboard
le tableau blanc

HIGHER EDUCATION

cafeteria
la cafétéria

campus
le campus

lecture hall
l'amphithéâtre *m*

lecturer
**le professeur / la
professeure d'université**

library
la bibliothèque

student
l'étudiant *m* /
l'étudiante *f*

131

Office hours tend to be from 8.30 a.m. to 6 p.m. Many businesses will have a lunch break of 1-2 hours, though this is now less common in larger French cities.

YOU MIGHT SAY/HEAR...

Can we arrange a meeting?
On peut fixer un rendez-vous ?

I have a meeting with...
J'ai un rendez-vous avec...

May I speak to...?
Je peux parler à...?

I'll email the files to you.
Je vous enverrai les documents par e-mail.

Who's calling?
Qui est au téléphone ?

Mr/Ms ... is on the phone.
M. / Mme ... est au téléphone.

Can I call you back?
Je peux vous rappeler ?

Here's my business card.
Voici ma carte de visite.

YOU SHOULD KNOW...

At lunchtime, eating at one's office desk rather than taking a break with colleagues is seen as unusual, even rude, by many French people.

VOCABULARY

manager
le gérant / la gérante

staff
le personnel

colleague
le collègue / la collègue

client
le client / la cliente

human resources
les ressources humaines *fpl*

accounts
la comptabilité

figures
les chiffres *mpl*

spreadsheet
la feuille de calcul

presentation
la présentation

report
le rapport

meeting
la réunion

conference call
la conférence téléphonique

video conference
la visioconférence

ink cartridge
la cartouche d'encre

inbox
la boîte de réception

file
le fichier

password
le mot de passe

to give a presentation
**faire une
présentation**

attachment
la pièce jointe

to type
taper

username
le nom d'utilisateur

to log on/off
**se connecter /
fermer la session**

to hold a meeting
tenir une réunion

to crash
tomber en panne

calculator
la calculatrice

desk
le bureau

desk lamp
la lampe de bureau

filing cabinet
le classeur

folder
la chemise

hole punch
la perforatrice

in/out tray
**la corbeille à
courrier**

laptop
**l'ordinateur
portable** *m*

notepad
le bloc-notes

paper clip
le trombone

photocopier
la photocopieuse

printer
l'imprimante *f*

ring binder
le classeur

scanner
le scanner

scissors
les ciseaux *mpl*

stapler
l'agrafeuse *f*

sticky notes
les post-it® *mpl*

sticky tape
le scotch®

swivel chair
le fauteuil pivotant

telephone
le téléphone

USB stick
la clé USB

Most banks are open during normal business hours from Monday to Friday, and some are also open on Saturday mornings, though this can vary.

YOU MIGHT SAY...

I'd like to...
J'aimerais...

... open an account.
... ouvrir un compte.

... apply for a loan/mortgage.
... demander un prêt / un prêt immobilier.

... register for online banking.
... m'inscrire aux services bancaires en ligne.

Is there a fee for this service?
Est-ce qu'il y a des frais ?

I need to cancel my debit/credit card.
Je dois résilier ma carte bancaire.

YOU MIGHT HEAR...

May I see your ID, please?
Votre pièce d'identité, s'il vous plaît.

How much would you like to withdraw/deposit?
Combien voulez-vous retirer / déposer ?

Could you enter your PIN, please?
Pouvez-vous taper votre code ?

You must fill out an application form.
Vous devez remplir un formulaire.

You must make an appointment.
Vous devez prendre rendez-vous.

There is a fee for this service.
Il y a des frais.

VOCABULARY

branch **l'agence** *f*	bank account **le compte en banque**	account number **le numéro de compte**
cashier **le guichetier / la guichetière**	current account **le compte courant**	bank statement **le relevé de compte**
online banking **les services bancaires en ligne** *mpl*	savings account **le compte d'épargne**	bank balance **le solde**

overdraft	loan	to repay
le découvert	le prêt	rembourser
bank transfer	mortgage	to withdraw
le virement bancaire	le prêt immobilier	retirer
chequebook	interest	to make a deposit
le carnet de chèques	les intérêts *mpl*	verser de l'argent
		sur un compte
currency	to borrow	
la devise	emprunter	to change money
		changer de l'argent

If using a foreign debit card whilst in France, most cash machines will give you the option of carrying out transactions in another language.

ATM
le distributeur de billets

banknotes
les billets de banque *mpl*

bureau de change
le bureau de change

debit/credit card
la carte de paiement / de crédit

exchange rate
le taux de change

safety deposit box
le coffre-fort

Opening hours for post offices will vary widely from place to place, so check what times the local branch opens and closes. Be aware that some postboxes will have one slot for local mail and one for destinations further afield.

YOU MIGHT SAY...

I'd like to send this first-class/ by airmail.
J'aimerais poster ceci en lettre prioritaire / par avion.

Can I get a certificate of postage, please?
Puis-je avoir une preuve de dépôt ?

How long will delivery take?
Ça va mettre combien de temps à arriver ?

I'd like a book of stamps, please.
Un carnet de timbres, s'il vous plaît.

YOU MIGHT HEAR...

Place it on the scales, please.
Posez-le sur la balance, s'il vous plaît.

What are the contents?
Qu'est-ce qu'il y a à l'intérieur ?

What is the value of this parcel?
Quelle est la valeur de ce colis ?

Would you like a certificate of postage?
Voulez-vous une preuve de dépôt ?

How many stamps do you require?
Vous avez besoin de combien de timbres ?

VOCABULARY

address **l'adresse** f	green letter **la lettre verte**	airmail **la poste aérienne**
first-class letter **la lettre prioritaire**	courier **le coursier**	to post **poster**
second-class letter **la lettre écopli**	mail **le courrier**	to send **envoyer**

YOU SHOULD KNOW...

As well as first- and second-class stamps, it is possible to buy a "green letter" stamp for sending letters within France as an eco-friendly alternative.

box
la boîte

envelope
l'enveloppe *f*

letter
la lettre

package
le colis

padded envelope
l'enveloppe à bulles *f*

postal worker
**le facteur /
la factrice**

postbox
la boîte aux lettres

postcard
la carte postale

stamp
le timbre

138

How do I get to the city centre?
Comment puis-je aller au centre-ville ?

I'd like to visit...
J'aimerais visiter...

I need to go to...
Il faut que j'aille à...

What are the opening hours?
Quelles sont les heures d'ouverture ?

It's open between ... and...
C'est ouvert entre ... et...

It's closed on Mondays.
C'est fermé le lundi.

PLACES OF IMPORTANCE

café
le café

cathedral
la cathédrale

church
l'église *f*

conference centre
le palais des congrès

courthouse
le tribunal

fire station
la caserne de pompiers

fountain
la fontaine

hospital
l'hôpital *m*

hotel
l'hôtel *m*

laundrette
la laverie

library
la bibliothèque

mosque
la mosquée

office block
l'immeuble de bureaux *m*

park
le parc

playground
l'aire de jeux *f*

police station
le commissariat

synagogue
la synagogue

town hall
la mairie

LEISURE | LES LOISIRS

A day trip, a break away, a night out, maybe even a night in – we all like to spend our free time differently. It's also a common topic of conversation with friends and colleagues; who doesn't like talking about holidays, hobbies, and how they like to hang out?

tent
la tente

guy rope
la corde de tente

flysheet
le double toit

groundsheet
le tapis de sol

tent peg
le piquet

YOU MIGHT SAY...

What would you like to do?
Que voulez-vous faire ?

What do you do in your spare time?
Que faites-vous pendant votre temps libre ?

Have you got any hobbies?
Avez-vous des passe-temps ?

Do you enjoy...?
Est-ce que vous aimez...?

How did you get into...?
Comment vous vous êtes mis à...?

Are you sporty/creative/musical?
Êtes-vous sportif / créatif / musicien ?

Are you going on holiday this year?
Vous partez en vacances cette année ?

YOU MIGHT HEAR...

My hobbies are...
Mes passe-temps sont...

I like...
J'aime...

I really enjoy it.
J'aime beaucoup.

It's not for me.
Ce n'est pas fait pour moi.

I'm going on holiday.
Je pars en vacances.

I am sporty/creative/musical.
Je suis sportif / créatif / musicien.

I do/don't have a lot of spare time.
J'ai / Je n'ai pas beaucoup de temps libre.

VOCABULARY

holiday **les vacances** *fpl*	fun **amusant**	to pass the time **passer le temps**
spare time **le temps libre**	boring **ennuyeux**	to relax **se détendre**
activity **l'activité** *f*	to be interested in **s'intéresser à**	to enjoy **apprécier**
hobby/pastime **le passe-temps**	to be keen on **être passionné par**	to be bored **s'ennuyer**

cooking
la cuisine

DIY
le bricolage

gaming
les jeux vidéo *mpl*

gardening
le jardinage

jogging
le jogging

listening to music
écouter de la musique

reading
la lecture

shopping
le shopping

sports
le sport

travelling
le voyage

walking
la marche

watching TV/films
regarder la télévision / des films

France is one of the most popular tourist destinations in the world – given the wealth of sightseeing opportunities it offers, it's easy to see why.

YOU MIGHT SAY...

How much is it to get in?
À combien est l'entrée ?

Is there a discount for students?
Est-ce qu'il y a un tarif réduit pour les étudiants ?

Where is the tourist office?
Où est l'office de tourisme ?

Are there sightseeing tours?
Est-ce qu'il y a des circuits touristiques ?

Are there audio guides available?
Est-ce qu'il y a des audio-guides ?

YOU MIGHT HEAR...

Entry costs...
L'entrée est à...

There is/isn't a discount available.
Il y a un / Il n'y a pas de tarif réduit.

The tourist office is located...
L'office de tourisme est...

You can book a guided tour.
Vous pouvez réserver une visite guidée.

Audio guides are/are not available.
Il y a des / Il n'y a pas d'audioguides.

VOCABULARY

tourist
**le touriste /
la touriste**

tourist attraction
**l'attraction
touristique** f

excursion
l'excursion f

nature reserve
la réserve naturelle

historic site
le site historique

guided tour
la visite guidée

audio guide
l'audio-guide m

to visit
visiter

to see
voir

YOU SHOULD KNOW...

Some cultural and historical sites, such as museums, art galleries and chateaus, are closed on certain days of the week (usually a Monday or Tuesday).

art gallery
la galerie d'art

camera
l'appareil photo *m*

castle
le château

cathedral
la cathédrale

city map
**le plan du
centre-ville**

gardens
le jardin public

guidebook
le guide

monument
le monument

museum
le musée

sightseeing bus
le bus touristique

tour guide
**le guide touristique /
la guide touristique**

tourist office
l'office de tourisme *m*

When it comes to nightlife in France's towns and cities, check the local tourist office for information on local events and venues. Why not get personal recommendations on bars and clubs from residents, too?

YOU MIGHT SAY...

What is there to do at night?
Qu'est-ce qu'on peut faire le soir ?

What's on at the cinema/theatre?
Qu'est-ce qu'il y a au cinéma / théâtre ?

Where are the best bars/clubs?
Où sont les meilleurs bars / meilleures boîtes ?

Do you want to go for a drink?
Vous voulez aller boire un verre ?

Do you want to go and see a film/show?
Vous voulez aller voir un film / spectacle ?

Are there tickets for...?
Est-ce qu'il y a des billets pour...?

Two seats in the stalls/balcony, please.
Deux places dans l'orchestre / au balcon, s'il vous plaît.

What time does it start?
Ça commence à quelle heure ?

I enjoyed myself.
Je me suis bien amusé.

YOU MIGHT HEAR...

The nightlife is/isn't great around here.
Il y a / Il n'y a pas une super vie nocturne par ici.

My favourite bar/club is...
Mon bar préféré / Ma boîte préférée, c'est...

I'm going for a few drinks/to the theatre.
Je vais boire un verre / au théâtre.

There's a film/show I'd like to see.
Il y a un film / spectacle que j'aimerais voir.

There are tickets left.
Il reste des billets.

There are no tickets left.
Il ne reste pas de billets.

It begins at 7 o'clock.
Ça commence à 19h.

Please turn off your mobile phones.
Veuillez éteindre vos téléphones portables.

Did you have a good night?
Vous avez passé une bonne soirée ?

a drink	film	to see a show
un verre	**le film**	**voir un spectacle**
nightlife	festival	to watch a film
la vie nocturne	**le festival**	**regarder un film**
party	box office	to go dancing
la fête	**la billetterie**	**aller danser**
show	to socialize	to order food/drinks
le spectacle	**rencontrer des gens**	**commander à**
		manger / au bar
play	to enjoy oneself	
la pièce	**s'amuser**	

YOU SHOULD KNOW...

Many bars and restaurants in French towns and cities have outdoor terraces ideal for people-watching; however, waiters can object to customers rearranging tables and chairs, so it's best to ask them to do it for you.

ballet
le ballet

bar
le bar

carnival
le carnaval

casino
le casino

cinema
le cinéma

comedy show
le spectacle comique

concert
le concert

funfair
la fête foraine

musical
la comédie musicale

nightclub
la boîte de nuit

opera
l'opéra *m*

restaurant
le restaurant

theatre
le théâtre

France regularly tops the tables for the world's most visited country, and there's a vast range of accommodation available for visitors, from high-end hotels to cosy bed and breakfasts ("chambres d'hôte").

YOU MIGHT SAY...

Have you got rooms available?
Avez-vous des chambres libres ?

How much is it per night?
C'est combien par nuit ?

Is breakfast included?
Est-ce que le petit-déjeuner est inclus ?

Is there a city tax?
Est-ce qu'il y a une taxe de séjour ?

I'd like to check in/out, please.
J'aimerais prendre / quitter ma chambre.

What time is breakfast served?
Le petit-déjeuner est servi à quelle heure ?

I have a reservation.
J'ai une réservation.

I'd like to book a single/double room, please.
J'aimerais réserver une chambre simple / double.

What time do I have to check out?
À quelle heure dois-je partir ?

Could I upgrade my room?
Puis-je surclasser ma chambre ?

I need fresh towels/more soap for my room.
J'ai besoin de serviettes propres / de savon dans ma chambre.

I'm in room number...
Je suis dans la chambre...

I've lost my key.
J'ai perdu la clé.

I'd like to make a complaint.
Je voudrais faire une réclamation.

YOU SHOULD KNOW...

When checking in to your hotel, you may be expected to fill out a registration form ("fiche d'hôtel") and provide your passport number.

We have/don't have rooms available.
Nous avons des chambres libres. / Nous n'avons pas de chambres libres.

Our rates are...
Nos prix sont...

Breakfast is/is not included.
Le petit-déjeuner est / n'est pas inclus.

Breakfast is served at...
Le petit-déjeuner est servi à...

May I have your room number, please?
Pouvez-vous me donner votre numéro de chambre ?

May I see your documents, please?
Votre réservation, s'il vous plaît.

You may check in after...
Vous pouvez arriver à partir de...

You must check out before...
Vous devez partir avant...

VOCABULARY

bed and breakfast
la chambre d'hôte

full board
la pension complète

half board
la demi-pension

room service
le room service

wake-up call
le réveil par téléphone

room number
le numéro de chambre

per person per night
par personne et par nuit

to check in
s'enregistrer

to check out
régler sa note

to order room service
commander quelque chose au room service

corridor
le couloir

"do not disturb" sign
le panneau "prière de ne pas déranger"

double room
la chambre pour deux personnes

key card
la carte magnétique

minibar
le minibar

porter
**le bagagiste /
la bagagiste**

reception
la réception

receptionist
**le réceptionniste /
la réceptionniste**

safe
le coffre-fort

single room
**la chambre pour une
personne**

toiletries
**les affaires de
toilette** *fpl*

twin room
la chambre à deux lits

There are a vast number of campsites all around France, and there are also options for wild camping ("camping sauvage"). Check what the local and national restrictions are before you set off on your trip.

YOU MIGHT SAY...

Is it OK to camp in this area?
Est-ce que je peux camper ici ?

Have you got spaces available?
Avez-vous des emplacements libres ?

I'd like to book for ... nights.
J'aimerais réserver pour ... nuits.

How much is it per night?
C'est combien par nuit ?

Where is the toilet/shower block?
Où est le bloc sanitaire ?

Is the water drinkable?
Est-ce que l'eau est potable ?

YOU MIGHT HEAR...

You can/can't put your tent up here.
Vous pouvez / ne pouvez pas monter votre tente ici.

We have/don't have spaces available.
Nous avons / n'avons pas d'emplacements libres.

It costs ... per night.
C'est ... par nuit.

The toilets/showers are located...
Les toilettes / sanitaires sont...

The water is/is not drinkable.
L'eau est / n'est pas potable.

VOCABULARY

campsite
le camping

chalet
le chalet

summer camp
la colonie de vacances

pitch
l'emplacement *m*

electricity hook-up
le branchement électrique

toilet/shower block
le bloc sanitaire

camper
le campeur / la campeuse

caravanner
le caravanier / la caravanière

to camp
camper

to pitch a tent	to take down a tent	to go caravanning
monter une tente	**démonter une tente**	**partir en caravane**

If you plan on caravanning in France, be aware that taking a caravan on the "autoroute" (motorway) will incur extra toll charges.

air bed
le matelas pneumatique

camping stove
le réchaud de camping

caravan
la caravane

cool box
la glacière

matches
les allumettes *fpl*

motorhome
le camping-car

sleeping bag
le sac de couchage

tent
la tente

torch
la lampe torche

France has over 2,000 miles of varying coastline, from rocky cliffs to fine sandy beaches. The south-west coast is renowned as a popular destination for surfers, whilst the south is home to the Riviera and some of France's most well-known beach resorts.

YOU MIGHT SAY...

Is there a good beach nearby?
Est-ce qu'il y a une plage agréable près d'ici ?

Is swimming permitted?
La baignade est-elle autorisée ?

Is the water cold?
L'eau est-elle froide ?

Can we hire...?
Est-ce qu'on peut louer...?

Help! Lifeguard!
À l'aide ! Au secours !

YOU MIGHT HEAR...

This is a public/private beach.
C'est une plage publique / privée.

Swimming is allowed/forbidden.
La baignade est autorisée / interdite.

Swimming is/is not supervised.
La baignade est / n'est pas surveillée.

The water is warm/cold/freezing!
L'eau est bonne / froide / gelée !

VOCABULARY

"No swimming" **"Baignade interdite"**	lifeguard post **le poste de secours**	to sunbathe **prendre un bain de soleil**
bathing zone **la zone de baignade**	suntan **le bronzage**	to swim **nager**

YOU SHOULD KNOW...

Public beaches are often monitored and may use a flag system to indicate bathing conditions:
Green – "bathing permitted and monitored"
Orange – "bathing permitted and monitored, but not recommended"
Red – "bathing forbidden and unmonitored".

sand
le sable

sea
la mer

waves
les vagues *fpl*

parasol
le parasol

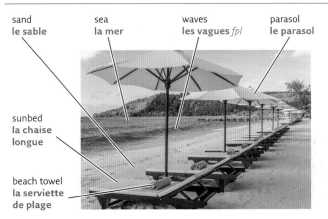

sunbed
**la chaise
longue**

beach towel
**la serviette
de plage**

GENERAL

beach ball
le ballon de plage

beach hut
la cabine de plage

bikini
le bikini

bucket and spade
le seau et la pelle

deckchair
le transat

flip-flops
les tongs *fpl*

flippers
les palmes *fpl*

promenade
la promenade

sandcastle
le château de sable

seashells
les coquillages *mpl*

seaweed
l'algue *f*

snorkel
le tuba

sunglasses
les lunettes de soleil
fpl

sunhat
le chapeau de soleil

suntan lotion
la crème solaire

swimming trunks
le short de bain

swimsuit
le maillot de bain

windbreak
le brise-vent

YOU MIGHT SAY...

I enjoy listening to music.
J'aime écouter de la musique.

I'm learning to play the...
J'apprends à jouer du / de la...

What kind of music do you like?
Quel genre de musique écoutes-tu ?

Is there a live music scene here?
Est-ce qu'il y a des concerts ici ?

YOU MIGHT HEAR...

I like/don't like...
J'aime / Je n'aime pas...

My favourite group is...
Mon groupe préféré, c'est...

There's a good music scene here.
Il y a une bonne scène musicale ici.

YOU SHOULD KNOW...

June 21st is Fête de la Musique (Music Day), celebrated worldwide and first established in France in 1982. Many free concerts and music events are held throughout the country on this date.

VOCABULARY

song	DJ	hip-hop
la chanson	**le DJ / la DJ**	**le hip hop**
album	CD	rap
l'album *m*	**le CD**	**le rap**
band/backing group	vinyl record	classical
le groupe	**le disque vinyle**	**classique**
live music/gig	microphone	folk
le concert	**le microphone**	**folk**
singer-songwriter	pop	electronic
le chanteur auteur compositeur /	**la pop**	**électronique**
la chanteuse auteur compositrice	rock	
	le rock	

to play an instrument
jouer d'un instrument

to listen to music
écouter de la musique

to stream music
écouter de la musique en streaming

to sing
chanter

to go to gigs
aller à des concerts

EQUIPMENT

Bluetooth® speaker
l'enceinte Bluetooth® *f*

earphones
les écouteurs *mpl*

headphones
le casque

soundbar
la barre de son

speakers
les haut-parleurs *mpl*

turntable
la platine

MUSICAL INSTRUMENTS

accordion
l'accordéon *m*

acoustic guitar
la guitare acoustique

bass drum
la grosse caisse

bass guitar
la guitare basse

cello
le violoncelle

clarinet
la clarinette

cymbals
les cymbales *fpl*

double bass
la contrebasse

electric guitar
la guitare électrique

flute
la flûte

harp
la harpe

keyboard
le clavier

mouth organ
l'harmonica *m*

piano
le piano

saxophone
le saxophone

snare drum
la caisse claire

trombone
le trombone

trumpet
la trompette

tuba
le tuba

violin
le violon

xylophone
le xylophone

GENERAL

choir
la chorale

conductor
**le chef d'orchestre /
la chef d'orchestre**

musician
**le musicien /
la musicienne**

orchestra
l'orchestre *m*

sheet music
la partition

singer
**le chanteur /
la chanteuse**

YOU MIGHT SAY...

Can I take photos here?
Je peux prendre des photos ici ?

Where can I print my photos?
Où est-ce que je peux imprimer mes photos ?

YOU MIGHT HEAR...

Photography isn't allowed.
Les photos ne sont pas autorisées.

Say cheese!
Souriez !

VOCABULARY

photographer
le photographe / la photographe

photo
la photo

selfie
le selfie

selfie stick
la perche à selfie

to take a photo/selfie
prendre une photo / un selfie

to zoom in
zoomer

camera lens
l'objectif photo *m*

compact camera
l'appareil photo compact *m*

drone
le drone

DSLR camera
l'appareil photo reflex numérique *m*

SD card
la carte SD

tripod
le trépied

Board game cafés where you can get together over a drink and a favourite board game make for great opportunities to use and improve your French!

What would you like to play?
À quoi voulez-vous jouer ?

What are the rules?
Quelles sont les règles ?

It's your turn.
C'est à toi.

Time's up!
Le temps est écoulé !

VOCABULARY

player
**le joueur /
la joueuse**

charades
les charades *fpl*

hide and seek
le cache-cache

solitaire
le solitaire

poker
le poker

hand (in cards)
le jeu

video game
le jeu vidéo

games console
la console de jeux

game controller
la manette de jeu

joystick
le joystick

virtual reality headset
**la casque de réalité
virtuelle**

crossword
les mots croisés *mpl*

sudoku
le sudoku

skittles
le jeu de quilles

to play
jouer

to roll the dice
jeter les dés

to win
gagner

to lose
perdre

YOU SHOULD KNOW...

The French game "pétanque" is a form of bowls originally played in Provence; today, it's played throughout the country and you can find petanque organizations right across the world.

backgammon
le backgammon

board game
le jeu de société

bowling
le bowling

cards
les cartes *fpl*

chess
les échecs *mpl*

counters
les pions *mpl*

darts
les fléchettes *fpl*

dice
le dé

dominoes
les dominos *mpl*

draughts
les dames *fpl*

jigsaw puzzle
le puzzle

petanque
la pétanque

163

There has been a growing interest in arts and crafts over recent years in France, with more and more craft fairs appearing across the country. Painting holidays are also becoming increasingly popular.

VOCABULARY

handicrafts **les objets artisanaux** *mpl*	amateur **l'amateur** *m* / **l'amatrice** *f*	to sketch **esquisser**
		to sew **coudre**
craft fair **l'exposition-vente d'artisanat** *f*	dressmaker **le couturier / la couturière**	to knit **tricoter**
artist **l'artiste** *m* / **l'artiste** *f*	to paint **peindre**	to be creative **être créatif**

GENERAL CRAFTS

embroidery
la broderie

jewellery-making
fabriquer des bijoux

model-making
le modélisme

papercrafts
la création en papier

pottery
la poterie

woodwork
la menuiserie

canvas
la toile

easel
le chevalet

ink
l'encre *f*

oil paint
la peinture à l'huile

paintbrush
le pinceau

palette
la palette

paper
le papier

pastels
les pastels *mpl*

pen
le stylo

pencil
le crayon

sketchpad
le carnet de croquis

watercolours
les couleurs pour aquarelle *fpl*

ball of wool
la pelote de laine

buttons
les boutons *mpl*

crochet hook
l'aiguille à crochet *f*

fabric
le tissu

fabric scissors
les ciseaux de couture *mpl*

knitting needles
les aiguilles à tricoter *fpl*

needle and thread
du fil et une aiguille

pins
les épingles *fpl*

safety pin
l'épingle à nourrice *f*

sewing basket
la boîte à couture

sewing machine
la machine à coudre

tape measure
le mètre ruban

SPORT | LE SPORT

Be it football or rugby, cycling or skiing, France has an impressive sporting history. There are hundreds of sports and fitness clubs, plus events across the country that you can get involved with, either as a player or as a spectator. You may be looking to participate in a sport or head to the gym, or you may simply want to chat about how "les Bleus" are getting on.

football pitch
le terrain de football

centre circle
le cercle central

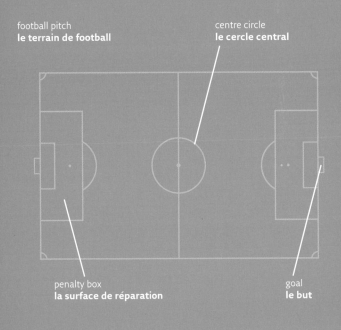

penalty box
la surface de réparation

goal
le but

YOU MIGHT SAY...

I like keeping active.
J'aime être actif.

Where is...?
Où se trouve...?

Where is the nearest...?
Où est le / la ... le / la plus proche ?

I train ... times per week.
Je m'entraîne ... fois par semaine.

I play rugby/hockey.
Je joue au rugby / hockey.

I'd like to book...
Je voudrais réserver...

YOU MIGHT HEAR...

There's a ... nearby.
Il y a ... près d'ici.

Do you do any sports?
Est-ce que vous faites du sport ?

Where/When do you train?
Où / Quand vous entraînez-vous ?

Do you follow any sports?
Est-ce que vous suivez un sport ?

What's your favourite team?
Quelle est votre équipe préférée ?

I'm a fan of...
Je suis un fan de...

VOCABULARY

tournament
le tournoi

competition
la compétition

league
la ligue

champion
le champion / la championne

competitor
le concurrent / la concurrente

teammate
le coéquipier / la coéquipière

coach
l'entraîneur *m* **/ l'entraîneuse** *f*

manager
le directeur sportif / la directrice sportive

match
le match

points
les points *mpl*

to coach
entraîner

to compete
participer

to score
marquer

to win
gagner

to lose
perdre

to draw
faire match nul

leisure centre
le centre sportif

medal
la médaille

official
l'officiel *m* /
l'officielle *f*

podium
le podium

referee
l'arbitre *m* /
l'arbitre *f*

scoreboard
**le tableau des
scores**

spectators
les spectateurs *mpl*

sportsperson
**le sportif /
la sportive**

stadium
le stade

stands
la tribune

team
l'équipe *f*

trophy
le trophée

YOU MIGHT SAY...

I'd like to join the gym.
J'aimerais m'inscrire à la salle de sport.

I'd like to book a class.
J'aimerais m'inscrire à un cours.

What are the facilities like?
Quels sont les équipements ?

What classes can you do here?
Quel genre de cours donnez-vous ici ?

YOU MIGHT HEAR...

Are you a member here?
Est-ce que vous êtes membre ici ?

Would you like to book an induction?
Voulez-vous vous inscrire à un bilan sportif ?

What time would you like to book for?
À quel moment voulez-vous vous inscrire ?

VOCABULARY

gym
la salle de sport

gym instructor
le professeur de fitness / la professeure de fitness

personal trainer
l'entraîneur personnel *m /* **l'entraîneuse personnelle** *f*

gym membership
l'abonnement à la salle de sport *m*

exercise class
le cours de remise en forme

Pilates
le Pilates

yoga
le yoga

press-ups
les pompes *fpl*

sit-ups
les abdominaux *mpl*

running
la course

to exercise
faire du sport

to keep fit
se maintenir en forme

to go for a run
aller courir

to go to the gym
aller à la salle de sport

YOU SHOULD KNOW...

Some gyms may expect you to continue paying for the duration of your membership even if you are unable to continue attending.

changing room
le vestiaire

cross trainer
le vélo elliptique

dumbbell
l'haltère *m*

exercise bike
**le vélo
d'appartement**

gym ball
le ballon de gym

kettlebell
le kettlebell

locker
le casier

rowing machine
le rameur

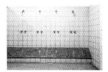

showers
les douches *fpl*

skipping rope
la corde à sauter

treadmill
le tapis roulant

weightlifting bench
**le banc de
musculation**

Football is the most widely played sport in France. The national team have been World Cup and European Championship winners.

YOU MIGHT SAY...

Are you going to watch the match?
Est-ce que vous allez regarder le match ?

What's the score?
Quel est le score ?

Foul!
Faute !

YOU MIGHT HEAR...

I'm watching the match.
Je regarde le match.

The score is...
Le score est de...

Go on!
Allez !

VOCABULARY

defender
le défenseur / la défenseure

striker
l'attaquant *m* / **l'attaquante** *f*

substitute
le remplaçant / la remplaçante

kick-off
le coup d'envoi

half-time
la mi-temps

full-time
la fin du match

extra time
les prolongations *fpl*

added time
le temps additionnel

free kick
le coup franc

header
le coup de tête

save
l'arrêt (du ballon) *m*

foul
la faute

offside
hors jeu

penalty
le penalty

penalty box
la surface de réparation

to play football
jouer au football

to kick
donner un coup de pied

to pass the ball
faire une passe

to score a goal
marquer un but

assistant referee
**le juge de ligne /
la juge de ligne**

football
le ballon de foot

football boots
**les chaussures de
foot** *fpl*

football match
le match de football

football pitch
le terrain de football

football player
**le footballeur /
la footballeuse**

goal
le but

goalkeeper
**le gardien de but /
la gardienne de but**

goalkeeper's gloves
**les gants de gardien
de but** *mpl*

shin pads
les protège-tibias *mpl*

whistle
le sifflet

yellow/red card
**le carton jaune /
rouge**

Although it is played across the country, rugby is particularly popular in the south of France. Rugby union is more widely known, but rugby league is also played.

VOCABULARY

rugby league/union
le rugby à treize / quinze

wheelchair rugby
le rugby fauteuil

forward
l'avant *m /*
l'avant *f*

back
l'arrière *m /*
l'arrière *f*

try
l'essai *m*

conversion
la transformation

penalty kick
la pénalité

drop goal
le drop

pass
la passe

headguard
le casque

mouthguard
le protège-dents

to play rugby
jouer au rugby

to tackle
plaquer

to score a try
marquer un essai

rugby
le rugby

rugby ball
le ballon de rugby

rugby field
le terrain de rugby

(rugby) goalposts
les poteaux de but (de rugby) *mpl*

rugby player
le joueur de rugby /
la joueuse de rugby

scrum
la mêlée

Interest in basketball in France has grown rapidly over the last few decades. France is now one of the main exporters of foreign players to the American NBA.

VOCABULARY

wheelchair basketball **le basket fauteuil**	free throw **le lancer franc**	to dribble **dribbler**
backboard **le panneau**	to play basketball **jouer au basket-ball**	to block **contrer**
layup **le tir en course**	to catch **attraper**	to mark **marquer**
slam dunk **le dunk**	to throw **lancer**	to score a basket **marquer un panier**

basket
le panier

basketball
le ballon de basket-ball

basketball court
le terrain

basketball game
le (match de) basket-ball

basketball player
le basketteur / la basketteuse

basketball shoes
les chaussures de basket *fpl*

VOCABULARY

ace **l'ace** *m*	rally **l'échange** *m*	to play badminton/ squash **jouer au badminton / squash**
serve **le service**	game, set and match **jeu, set et match**	
backhand **le revers**	singles **le simple**	to hit **frapper**
forehand **le coup droit**	doubles **le double**	to serve **servir**
fault **la faute**	top seed **la tête de série**	to break his/her serve **prendre le service de son adversaire**
net **le filet**	to play tennis **jouer au tennis**	

BADMINTON

badminton
le badminton

badminton racket
**la raquette de
badminton**

shuttlecock
le volant

SQUASH

squash
le squash

squash ball
la balle de squash

squash racket
**la raquette de
squash**

ball boy/girl
**le ramasseur
de balles / la
ramasseuse de balles**

line judge
**le juge de ligne /
la juge de ligne**

tennis
le tennis

tennis ball
la balle de tennis

tennis court
le court de tennis

tennis player
**le joueur de tennis /
la joueuse de tennis**

umpire
l'arbitre *m* / **l'arbitre** *f*

tennis racket
la raquette de tennis

umpire's chair
la chaise de l'arbitre

There are a whole range of water sports you can try out whilst in France, by the coast as well as inland. It's always advisable to seek out experienced instructors and source any appropriate safety equipment.

YOU MIGHT SAY...

I'm a keen swimmer.
Je suis un nageur passioné.

I'm not a strong swimmer.
Je ne suis pas un bon nageur.

Can I hire...?
Est-ce que je peux louer...

YOU MIGHT HEAR...

You can hire...
Vous pouvez louer...

You must wear a lifejacket.
Vous devez porter un gilet de sauvetage.

The water is deep/shallow.
L'eau est profonde / peu profonde.

VOCABULARY

swimming	lane	to swim
la natation	le couloir	nager
swimmer	length	to dive
le nageur /	la longueur	plonger
la nageuse		
	swimming lesson	to surf
diver	la leçon de natation	surfer
le plongeur /		
la plongeuse	diving	to paddle
	la plongée	pagayer
breaststroke		
la brasse	angling	to row
	la pêche à la ligne	ramer
backstroke		
le dos crawlé	angler	to sail
	le pêcheur /	naviguer
front crawl	la pêcheuse	
le crawl		to fish
	surfer	pêcher
butterfly	le surfeur /	
le papillon	la surfeuse	

armbands
les brassards *mpl*

diving board
le plongeoir

flippers
les palmes *fpl*

goggles
**les lunettes de
piscine** *fpl*

lifeguard
**le sauveteur /
la sauveteuse**

swimming cap
le bonnet de bain

swimming pool
la piscine

swimming trunks
le short de bain

swimsuit
le maillot de bain

bodyboarding
le bodyboard

canoeing
le canoë

jet ski®
le jet-ski

kayaking
le kayak

lifejacket
le gilet de sauvetage

oars
les avirons *mpl*

paddle
la pagaie

paddleboarding
le paddle

scuba diving
**la plongée
sous-marine**

snorkelling
**la plongée (avec
masque et tuba)**

surfboard
la planche de surf

surfing
le surf

waterskiing
le ski nautique

wetsuit
**la combinaison de
plongée**

windsurfing
la planche à voile

With the Alps to the east, the Pyrenees to the south, and the Massif Central in between, there are plenty of opportunities to try mountain and winter sports in France.

YOU MIGHT SAY...

Can I hire some skis?
Est-ce que je peux louer des skis ?

I'd like a skiing lesson, please.
J'aimerais prendre des cours de ski.

I can't ski very well.
Je ne skie pas très bien.

What are the snow conditions like?
Quels sont les conditions de ski ?

I've fallen.
Je suis tombé.

I've hurt myself.
Je me suis fait mal.

Help!
À l'aide !

YOU MIGHT HEAR...

You can hire skis here.
Vous pouvez louer des skis ici.

You can book a skiing lesson here.
Vous pouvez vous inscrire aux cours de ski ici.

Do you have much skiing experience?
Est-ce que vous avez déjà skié ?

The piste is open/closed today.
La piste est ouverte / fermée aujourd'hui.

The conditions are good/bad.
Les conditions sont bonnes / mauvaises.

There's an avalanche risk.
Il y a un risque d'avalanche.

Be careful.
Faites attention.

VOCABULARY

skier **le skieur / la skieuse**	ski lift **le remonte-pente**	mountain rescue service **le secours en montagne**
ski resort **la station de sports d'hiver**	ski instructor **le moniteur de ski / la monitrice de ski**	

first-aid kit
la trousse de premiers secours

snow
la neige

powder
la poudreuse

ice
la glace

avalanche
l'avalanche *f*

avalanche risk
le risque d'avalanches

to ski (off-piste)
skier (hors-piste)

to snowboard
faire du snowboard

to go sledging
faire de la luge

to go ice skating
faire du patin à glace

to go mountain climbing
faire de l'alpinisme

GENERAL

crampons
les crampons *mpl*

ice axe
le piolet

ice skates
les patins à glace *mpl*

ice skating
le patinage

rope
la corde

sledge
la luge

piste
la piste

salopettes
la salopette de ski

ski boots
les chaussures de ski *fpl*

ski gloves
les gants de ski *mpl*

ski goggles
les lunettes de ski *fpl*

ski helmet
le casque

ski jacket
le manteau de ski

ski poles
les bâtons de ski *mpl*

skis
les skis *mpl*

ski suit
la combinaison de ski

snowboard
la planche de snowboard

snowboarding boots
les chaussures de snowboard *fpl*

VOCABULARY

fight
le combat

boxer
**le boxeur /
la boxeuse**

fighter
**le combattant /
la combattante**

opponent
l'adversaire *m* /
l'adversaire *f*

featherweight
le poids plume

heavyweight
le poids lourd

punch
le coup de poing

knockout
le K.-O.

martial arts
les arts martiaux *mpl*

to box
boxer

to wrestle
faire de la lutte

to punch
**donner un coup de
poing**

to kick
**donner un coup de
pied**

to strike
frapper

to spar
s'entraîner

to knock out
assommer

YOU SHOULD KNOW...

Savate, or French boxing, is a combat sport that has its roots in street-fighting and self-defence techniques developed in French cities. Fighters use kicks and punches against opponents – the word "savate" comes from an old French word meaning "boot".

BOXING

boxing gloves
les gants de boxe *mpl*

boxing ring
le ring

boxing shoes
**les chaussures de
boxe** *fpl*

headguard
le casque

mouthguard
le protège-dents

punchbag
le sac de frappe

OTHER COMBAT SPORTS

fencing
l'escrime *f*

judo
le judo

karate
le karaté

kickboxing
le kick boxing

taekwondo
le taekwondo

wrestling
la lutte

VOCABULARY

race
la course

marathon
le marathon

starter's gun
le pistolet de départ

false start
le faux départ

runner
**le coureur /
la coureuse**

lane
le couloir

start line
le départ

finish line
la ligne d'arrivée

heat
l'éliminatoire f

final
la finale

sprint
le sprint

relay
la course de relais

triple jump
le triple saut

heptathlon
l'heptathlon m

decathlon
le décathlon

indoor athletics
**l'athlétisme en
salle** m

to do athletics
faire de l'athlétisme

to run
courir

to race
faire la course

to jump
sauter

to throw
lancer

YOU SHOULD KNOW...

The modern Olympic® movement was spearheaded by the French baron Pierre de Coubertin. He was the founder of the International Olympic Committee, and served as its second president.

athlete
l'athlète m /
l'athlète f

discus
le disque

high jump
le saut en hauteur

hurdles
la haie

javelin
le javelot

long jump
le saut en longueur

pole vault
le saut à la perche

running track
la piste

shot put
le lancer de poids

spikes
les chaussures à pointes *fpl*

stopwatch
le chronomètre

starting block
le starting-block

There are golf courses and clubs all over France. Golfing holidays are becoming increasingly popular, and you can hire any equipment you may need.

VOCABULARY

golfer
**le joueur de golf /
la joueuse de golf**

caddie
le caddie

golf course
le terrain de golf

fairway
le fairway

clubhouse
le pavillon

green
le green

bunker
le bunker

hole
le trou

hole-in-one
le trou en un

birdie
le birdie

handicap
le handicap

swing
le swing

over/under par
**au-dessus /
au-dessous du par**

to play golf
jouer au golf

to tee off
prendre le départ

golf bag
le sac de golf

golf ball
la balle de golf

golf buggy
la voiturette de golf

golf club
le club de golf

putter
le putter

tee
le té

American football
le football américain

archery
le tir à l'arc

baseball
le baseball

bowls
les boules *fpl*

climbing
l'escalade *f*

cricket
le cricket

fishing
la pêche

gymnastics
la gymnastique

handball
le handball

hockey
le hockey

horse racing
les courses hippiques *fpl*

ice hockey
le hockey sur glace

motorcycle racing
la course de motos

motor racing
**la course
automobile**

netball
le netball

shooting
le tir

showjumping
le concours hippique

skateboarding
le skate

snooker
le snooker

table tennis
le tennis de table

track cycling
le cyclisme sur piste

volleyball
le volley

water polo
le water-polo

weightlifting
l'haltérophilie *f*

HEALTH | LA SANTÉ

It's important to arrange appropriate cover for healthcare during your time in France - if you are a holidaymaker, ensure you have appropriate travel insurance in place. Healthcare for residents is funded by mandatory health insurance and provided by a system of public and private hospitals, doctors, and medical professionals.

first-aid kit
la trousse de secours

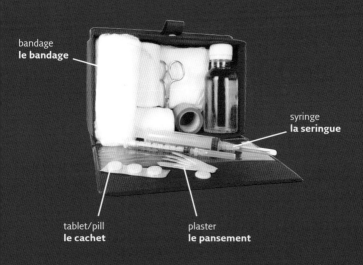

bandage
le bandage

syringe
la seringue

tablet/pill
le cachet

plaster
le pansement

The main phone numbers for emergency services in France are as follows: 15 – Samu (medical emergencies); 17 – Police / Gendarmes; 18 – Sapeurs Pompiers (fire brigade and medical emergencies). If in doubt, 112 is the Universal European Emergency Services number - it works from all phones, including mobiles, and will connect you to the appropriate emergency service.

YOU MIGHT SAY...

I don't feel well.
Je ne me sens pas bien.

I've hurt...
Je me suis fait mal à...

I'm going to be sick.
Je vais vomir.

I need to see a doctor.
Je dois voir un médecin.

I need to go to hospital.
Il faut que j'aille à l'hôpital.

Call an ambulance.
Appelez les secours.

YOU MIGHT HEAR...

What's wrong?
Quel est le problème ?

Where does it hurt?
Où avez-vous mal ?

What happened?
Qu'est-ce qui s'est passé ?

How long have you been feeling ill?
Depuis combien de temps avez-vous mal ?

YOU SHOULD KNOW...

The "Carte Vitale" is the national social security card, obligatory for residents aged 16 and above. Application procedures vary depending on residency and form of employment, so if you intend to obtain a "Carte Vitale", seek advice on the documentation you will need and the process to follow.

VOCABULARY

first aider	pain	illness
le secouriste /	**la douleur**	**la maladie**
la secouriste		

symptom	health insurance	to recover
le symptôme	**l'assurance maladie** *f*	**se remettre**

mental health	healthy	to look after
la santé mentale	**sain**	**s'occuper de**

treatment	to be ill/in pain	to treat
le traitement	**avoir mal**	**traiter**

doctor
**le médecin /
la médecin**

first-aid kit
**la trousse de
secours**

hospital
l'hôpital *m*

medicine
le médicament

nurse
l'infirmier *m* /
l'infirmière *f*

paramedic
**le secouriste /
la secouriste**

patient
**le patient /
la patiente**

pharmacist
**le pharmacien /
la pharmacienne**

pharmacy
la pharmacie

VOCABULARY

throat
la gorge

armpit
l'aisselle *f*

genitals
les organes génitaux
mpl

breast
le sein

eyelash
le cil

eyebrow
le sourcil

eyelid
la paupière

earlobe
le lobe de l'oreille

nostrils
les narines *fpl*

lips
les lèvres *fpl*

tongue
la langue

skin
la peau

(body) hair
les poils *mpl*

height
la taille

weight
le poids

BMI
l'IMC *m*

sense of hearing
l'ouïe *f*

sense of sight
la vue

sense of smell
l'odorat *m*

sense of taste
le goût

sense of touch
le toucher

balance
l'équilibre *m*

to see
voir

to smell
sentir

to hear
entendre

to touch
toucher

to taste
goûter

to stand
être debout

to walk
marcher

to lose one's balance
perdre l'équilibre

YOU SHOULD KNOW...

In French, possessive adjectives (for example, *my, his, their*) are not used to refer to one's body parts; reflexive verbs are used instead. For instance, "I washed my hands" is translated as "Je me suis lavé les mains".

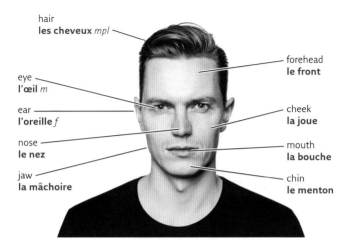

hair
les cheveux *mpl*

forehead
le front

eye
l'œil *m*

cheek
la joue

ear
l'oreille *f*

nose
le nez

mouth
la bouche

jaw
la mâchoire

chin
le menton

HAND

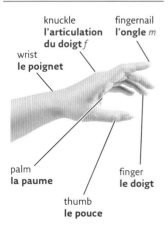

knuckle
**l'articulation
du doigt** *f*

fingernail
l'ongle *m*

wrist
le poignet

palm
la paume

finger
le doigt

thumb
le pouce

FOOT

big toe
**le gros
orteil**

toenail
**l'ongle
du pied** *m*

toe
**le doigt de
pied**

sole
**la plante
du pied**

heel
le talon

ankle
la cheville

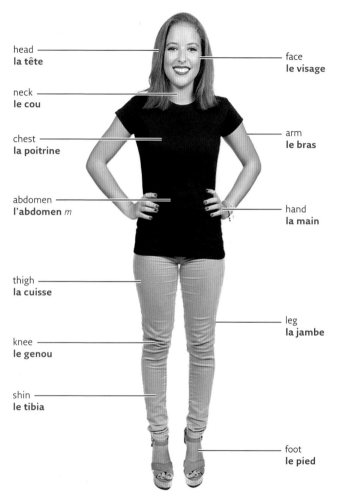

head
la tête

face
le visage

neck
le cou

chest
la poitrine

arm
le bras

abdomen
l'abdomen *m*

hand
la main

thigh
la cuisse

leg
la jambe

knee
le genou

shin
le tibia

foot
le pied

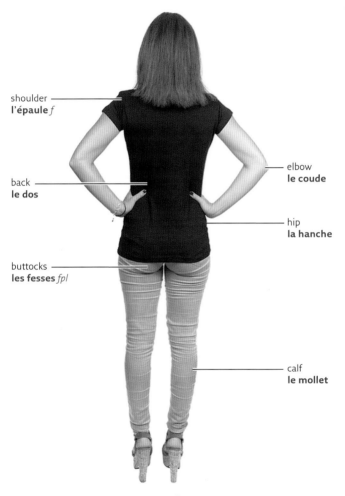

shoulder
l'épaule *f*

elbow
le coude

back
le dos

hip
la hanche

buttocks
les fesses *fpl*

calf
le mollet

Hopefully this is not vocabulary you will need very often, but it is useful to have the necessary terminology at your disposal, should the need arise.

VOCABULARY

organ
l'organe *m*

brain
le cerveau

heart
le cœur

lung
le poumon

liver
le foie

stomach
l'estomac *m*

kidney
le rein

intestines
les intestins *mpl*

bladder
la vessie

digestive system
le système digestif

respiratory system
le système respiratoire

blood
le sang

joint
l'articulation *f*

bone
l'os *m*

muscle
le muscle

nerve
le nerf

tendon
le tendon

tissue
le tissu

ligament
le ligament

cell
la cellule

artery
l'artère *f*

vein
la veine

oxygen
l'oxygène *m*

YOU SHOULD KNOW...

As in English, parts of the body feature often in common French expressions, such as:
"mettre sa langue dans sa poche" meaning "to keep quiet" (literally: to put your tongue in your pocket)
"casser les pieds à quelqu'un" meaning "to annoy or bore someone" (literally: to break someone's feet)
"être de bon / mauvais poil" meaning "to be in a good/bad mood" (literally: to be of good/bad hair).

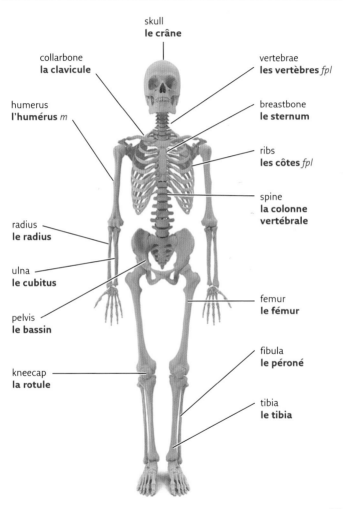

skull
le crâne

collarbone
la clavicule

vertebrae
les vertèbres *fpl*

humerus
l'humérus *m*

breastbone
le sternum

ribs
les côtes *fpl*

spine
la colonne vertébrale

radius
le radius

ulna
le cubitus

femur
le fémur

pelvis
le bassin

fibula
le péroné

kneecap
la rotule

tibia
le tibia

When attending a doctor's appointment, you will need to provide social security or insurance details. If you don't have this documentation to hand, you can fill in a "feuille de soin" (healthcare slip) at the doctor's surgery.

YOU MIGHT SAY...

I'd like to make an appointment.
Je voudrais prendre rendez-vous.

I have an appointment with Dr...
J'ai rendez-vous avec Dr...

I'm allergic to...
Je suis allergique à...

I take medication for...
Je prends des médicaments pour...

I've been feeling unwell.
Je ne me sens pas bien.

That hurts.
Ça fait mal.

YOU MIGHT HEAR...

Your appointment is at...
Votre rendez-vous est à...

The doctor/nurse will call you through.
Le médecin / L'infirmière va vous appeler.

What are your symptoms?
Quels sont vos symptômes ?

May I examine you?
Je pèux vous examiner ?

Tell me if that hurts.
Dites-moi si ça fait mal.

Do you have any allergies?
Est-ce que vous êtes allergique ?

Do you take any medication?
Prenez-vous des médicaments ?

Take two tablets twice a day.
Prenez deux cachets deux fois par jour.

You need to see a specialist.
Vous devriez voir un spécialiste.

VOCABULARY

appointment **le rendez-vous**	examination **l'examen médical** *m*	antibiotics **les antibiotiques** *mpl*
clinic **les consultations** *fpl*	test **le test**	the pill **la pilule**

sleeping pill
le somnifère

vaccination
le vaccin

to examine
examiner

prescription
l'ordonnance *f*

medication
le médicament

to be on medication
être sous médication

home visit
la visite à domicile

to make an appointment
prendre rendez-vous

blood pressure monitor
le tensiomètre

examination room
la salle d'examen

examination table
la table d'examen

GP
le médecin généraliste / la médecin généraliste

practice nurse
l'infirmier auxiliaire *m* **/ l'infirmière auxiliaire** *f*

stethoscope
le stéthoscope

syringe
la seringue

thermometer
le thermomètre

waiting room
la salle d'attente

YOU MIGHT SAY...

Can I book an emergency appointment?
Est-ce que je peux avoir une consultation d'urgence ?

I have toothache.
J'ai mal aux dents.

I have an abscess.
J'ai un abcès.

My filling has come out.
Mon plombage s'est décollé.

I've broken my tooth.
Je me suis cassé une dent.

My dentures are broken.
Mon dentier s'est cassé.

My gums are bleeding.
Mes gencives saignent.

YOU MIGHT HEAR...

We don't have any emergency appointments available.
Nous n'avons pas de consultation d'urgence disponible.

You need a new filling.
Vous avez besoin d'un nouveau plombage.

Unfortunately your tooth has to come out.
Malheureusement on doit vous arracher une dent.

You will need to make another appointment.
Vous devez prendre un autre rendez-vous.

VOCABULARY

check-up **l'examen dentaire** m	filling **le plombage**	toothache **la douleur dentaire**
molar **la molaire**	crown **la couronne**	abscess **l'abcès** m
incisor **l'incisive** f	root canal treatment **le traitement radiculaire**	to brush one's teeth **se brosser les dents**
canine **la canine**	extraction **l'extraction** f	to floss **se passer du fil dentaire entre les dents**
wisdom teeth **les dents de sagesse** fpl		

braces
l'appareil (dentaire)
m

dental floss
le fil dentaire

dental nurse
l'assistant dentaire
m / **l'assistante
dentaire** *f*

dentist
**le dentiste /
la dentiste**

dentist's chair
**le fauteuil de
dentiste**

dentist's drill
la fraise dentaire

dentures
le dentier

gums
les gencives *fpl*

mouthwash
le bain de bouche

teeth
les dents *fpl*

toothbrush
la brosse à dents

toothpaste
le dentifrice

Eye tests in France are usually carried out by ophthalmologists, who can provide you with a prescription for glasses or contact lenses to take to an optician.

YOU MIGHT SAY...

Can I book an appointment?
Est-ce que je peux prendre rendez-vous ?

My eyes are dry.
Mes yeux sont secs.

My eyes are sore.
J'ai mal aux yeux.

Do you repair glasses?
Faites-vous les réparations de lunettes ?

YOU MIGHT HEAR...

Your appointment is at...
Votre rendez-vous est à...

Look up/down/ahead.
Regardez en haut / en bas / devant vous.

You have perfect vision.
Vous avez une vision parfaite.

You need reading glasses.
Vous avez besoin de lunettes de lecture.

VOCABULARY

ophthalmologist
l'ophtalmologue m /
l'ophtalmologue f

reading glasses
les lunettes de lecture fpl

bifocals
les lunettes à double foyer fpl

hard/soft contact lenses
les lentilles de contact rigides / souples fpl

lens
la lentille

conjunctivitis
la conjonctivite

stye
l'orgelet m

blurred vision
la vision brouillée

cataracts
les cataractes fpl

short-sighted
myope

long-sighted
hypermétrope

visually impaired
malvoyant

blind
aveugle

colour-blind
daltonien

to wear glasses
porter des lunettes

to wear contacts
porter des lentilles de contact

contact lenses
les lentilles de contact

contact lens case
l'étui pour lentilles de contact *m*

eye chart
le tableau d'acuité visuelle

eye drops
le collyre

eye test
l'examen de la vue *m*

frames
la monture

glasses
les lunettes *fpl*

glasses case
l'étui à lunettes *m*

optician
l'opticien *m* /
l'opticienne *f*

THE HOSPITAL | L'HÔPITAL

Which ward is he/she in?
Il / Elle est dans quelle salle ?

When are visiting hours?
Quelles sont les heures de visite ?

He/She is in ward...
Il / Elle est dans la salle...

Visiting hours are between ... and...
Les heures de visite sont de ... à...

VOCABULARY

public hospital
l'hôpital *m*

private hospital
la clinique

physiotherapist
**le kinésithérapeute /
la kinésithérapeute**

radiographer
**le radiologue /
la radiologue**

surgeon
**le chirurgien /
la chirurgienne**

operation
l'opération *f*

scan
le scanner

defibrillator
le défibrillateur

intensive care
les soins intensifs *mpl*

diagnosis
le diagnostic

to undergo surgery
**subir une
intervention**

to be admitted/
discharged
laisser entrer / sortir

YOU SHOULD KNOW ...

There are both public and private hospitals available in France. However, many private hospitals work for the state healthcare system, and social and private health insurance should therefore cover most expenses.

A&E
**le service des
urgences**

ambulance
l'ambulance *f*

crutches
les béquilles *fpl*

drip
la perfusion

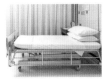

hospital bed
le lit d'hôpital

hospital trolley
le chariot roulant

monitor
l'écran *m*

operating theatre
la salle d'opération

oxygen mask
le masque à oxygène

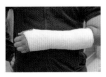

plaster cast
le plâtre

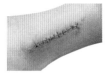

stitches
les points de suture
mpl

ward
la salle d'hôpital

wheelchair
le fauteuil roulant

X-ray
la radio

Zimmer frame®
le déambulateur

YOU MIGHT SAY...

Can you call an ambulance?
Pouvez-vous appeler les secours ?

I've had an accident.
J'ai eu un accident.

I've hurt...
Je me suis fait mal à...

I've broken/sprained...
Je me suis cassé / foulé...

I've cut/burnt myself.
Je me suis coupé / brûlé.

I've hit my head.
Je me suis cogné la tête.

YOU MIGHT HEAR...

Do you feel faint?
Vous sentez-vous faible ?

Do you feel sick?
Avez-vous envie de vomir ?

I'm calling an ambulance.
J'appelle les secours.

Where does it hurt?
Où avez-vous mal ?

Tell me what happened.
Dites-moi ce qui s'est passé.

YOU SHOULD KNOW...

In France, you need a doctor to confirm that you require an ambulance service, or you will be billed personally for ambulance costs. It is also possible to arrange a "véhicule sanitaire léger" (patient transportation vehicle) for travel to non-emergency medical appointments.

VOCABULARY

accident
l'accident *m*

pulse
le pouls

concussion
la commotion

fall
la chute

dislocation
le déboîtement

sprain
la foulure

scar
la cicatrice

whiplash
le coup du lapin

swelling
l'enflure *f*

first aid
les premiers secours
mpl

recovery position
la position latérale de sécurité

CPR
la RCP

to injure oneself
se blesser

to break one's arm
se casser le bras

to be unconscious
être inconscient

to fall
tomber

to twist one's ankle
se tordre la cheville

to take his/her pulse
prendre son pouls

INJURIES

blister
l'ampoule *f*

bruise
le bleu

burn
la brûlure

cut
la coupure

fracture
la fracture

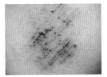

graze
l'éraflure *f*

splinter
l'écharde *f*

sting
la piqûre

sunburn
le coup de soleil

antiseptic
l'antiseptique *m*

bandage
le bandage

dressing
le pansement

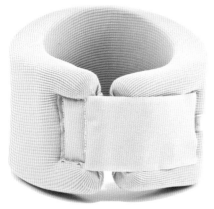

ice pack
la poche de glace

ointment
la pommade

neck brace
la minerve

plaster
le pansement

sling
l'écharpe *f*

tweezers
la pince à épiler

YOU MIGHT SAY...

I have a cold/the flu.
J'ai un rhume / la grippe.

I have a sore stomach.
J'ai mal au ventre.

I'm going to be sick.
Je vais vomir.

I'm asthmatic/diabetic.
Je fais de l'asthme / du diabète.

YOU MIGHT HEAR...

You should go to the doctor.
Vous devriez aller chez le médecin.

You need to rest.
Vous avez besoin de repos.

Do you need anything?
Avez-vous besoin de quelque chose ?

VOCABULARY

heart attack
la crise cardiaque

stroke
l'attaque *f*

infection
l'infection *f*

ear infection
l'otite *f*

fever
la fièvre

virus
le virus

chicken pox
la varicelle

rash
l'éruption cutanée *f*

stomach bug
la gastroentérite

food poisoning
l'intoxication alimentaire *f*

vomiting
les vomissements *mpl*

nausea
la nausée

diarrhoea
la diarrhée

constipation
la constipation

diabetes
le diabète

epilepsy
l'épilepsie *f*

asthma
l'asthme *m*

dizziness
le vertige

inhaler
l'inhalateur *m*

insulin
l'insuline *f*

period pain
les douleurs menstruelles *fpl*

to have high/low blood pressure
faire de l'hypertension / l'hypotension

to cough
tousser

to sneeze
éternuer

to vomit
vomir

to faint
s'évanouir

If you plan to have your baby in France, you will be referred to a gynaecologist who will be your principal contact during the pregnancy and who will advise on maternity hospitals and midwives. If you are travelling while pregnant, make sure you have appropriate travel insurance in place.

YOU MIGHT SAY...

I'm (six months) pregnant.
Je suis enceinte (de six mois).

My partner/wife is pregnant.
Ma compagne / femme est enceinte.

I'm/She's having contractions every ... minutes.
J'ai / Elle a des contractions toutes les ... minutes.

My/Her waters have broken.
J'ai / Elle a perdu les eaux.

I want an epidural.
Je veux une péridurale.

YOU MIGHT HEAR...

How far along are you?
Vous êtes enceinte de combien de mois ?

How long is it between contractions?
Combien de temps y a-t-il entre vos contractions ?

May I examine you?
Je peux vous examiner ?

Push!
Poussez !

VOCABULARY

pregnant woman
la femme enceinte

newborn
le nouveau-né / la nouveau-née

foetus
le fœtus

uterus
l'utérus m

cervix
le col de l'utérus

labour
le travail

gas and air
le gaz analgésique

epidural
la péridurale

birth plan
le projet d'accouchement

delivery
l'accouchement m

Caesarean section
la césarienne

miscarriage
la fausse couche

due date
**la date
d'accouchement**

morning sickness
la nausée matinale

stillborn
mort-né

to fall pregnant
tomber enceinte

to be in labour
être en travail

to give birth
accoucher

to miscarry
**faire une fausse
couche**

to breast-feed
allaiter

A full-term pregnancy in France is classed as 40 weeks and 6 days, as opposed to 39 weeks and 6 days. It is also common for parents to find out the baby's sex before birth, so let your health professionals know if you'd prefer a surprise!

incubator
la couveuse

labour suite
**la salle
d'accouchement**

midwife
la sage-femme

pregnancy test
le test de grossesse

sonographer
l'échographiste *m* /
l'échographiste *f*

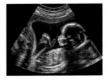

ultrasound
l'échographie *f*

Alternative therapies are popular in France, but not all are eligible for social security cover, so it is worth researching which treatments can be covered by standard insurance.

VOCABULARY

therapist **le thérapeute / la thérapeute**	acupuncturist **l'acupuncteur** *m* / **l'acupunctrice** *f*	reiki **le reiki**
masseur **le masseur**	reflexologist **le réflexologue / la réflexologue**	mindfulness **la pleine conscience**
masseuse **la masseuse**	remedy **le remède**	to massage **masser**
chiropractor **le chiropracteur** *m* / **la chiropractrice** *f*		to meditate **méditer**

YOU SHOULD KNOW...

Homeopathy is fairly widely accepted within the French healthcare system, and it is usually possible to find a wide range of homeopathic remedies in French pharmacies.

GENERAL

essential oil
l'huile essentielle *f*

herbal medicine
la phytothérapie

homeopathy
l'homéopathie *f*

acupuncture
l'acupuncture *f*

chiropractic
la chiropraxie

hypnotherapy
l'hypnothérapie *f*

massage
le massage

meditation
la méditation

osteopathy
l'ostéopathie *f*

reflexology
la réflexologie

thalassotherapy
la thalassothérapie

traditional Chinese
medicine
**la médecine
traditionnelle
chinoise**

If you intend to travel to France from the UK with your pet, they must be microchipped and vaccinated against rabies, and have a pet passport. Dogs must get a tapeworm treatment from a vet 12–24 hours before returning to the UK.

YOU MIGHT SAY...

My dog has been hurt.
Mon chien a été blessé.

I have to book a tapeworm treatment for my dog.
Je dois réserver un traitement vermifuge pour mon chien.

YOU MIGHT HEAR...

What seems to be the problem?
Quel est le problème ?

Is your pet microchipped?
Est-ce que votre animal de compagnie est pucé ?

VOCABULARY

vet
**le vétérinaire /
la vétérinaire**

pet
**l'animal de
compagnie** *m*

flea
la puce

tick
la tique

pet passport
**le passeport pour
animal domestique**

quarantine
la quarantaine

microchip
la puce

to vaccinate
vacciner

to worm
traiter contre les vers

to microchip
pucer

to spay/neuter
stériliser

to put down
piquer

E-collar
**la collerette
vétérinaire**

flea collar
le collier antipuces

pet carrier
**le panier de
transport**

PLANET EARTH | LA PLANÈTE TERRE

France's varied, colourful and dramatic landscape makes it a fantastic place to explore for anyone who loves the great outdoors, as well as offering a wealth of biodiversity. There are over 100,000 km of trails and footpaths that criss-cross the country, offering walkers plenty of opportunities to discover the French countryside for themselves. Numerous nature reserves and natural marine parks can be found throughout metropolitan France and its overseas territories too.

parrot
le perroquet

beak
le bec

tail
la queue

claw
la griffe

Is there a park/nature reserve nearby?
Est-ce qu'il y a un parc / une réserve naturelle près d'ici ?

What is the scenery like?
À quoi ressemble le paysage ?

The scenery is beautiful/rugged.
Le paysage est magnifique / sauvage.

I'd recommend visiting...
Je vous conseille d'aller à...

This is a protected area.
C'est une aire zone protégée.

VOCABULARY

animal l'animal *m*	paw la patte	beak le bec
bird l'oiseau *m*	hoof le sabot	cold-blooded à sang froid
fish le poisson	snout le museau	warm-blooded à sang chaud
species l'espèce *f*	mane la crinière	to bark aboyer
zoo le zoo	tail la queue	to purr ronronner
nature reserve la réserve naturelle	claw la griffe	to growl grogner
scenery le paysage	horn la corne	to chirp pépier
fur la fourrure	feather la plume	to buzz bourdonner
wool la laine	wing l'aile *f*	to roar rugir

France has one of the highest ratios of pet ownership in Europe. Hotels will often quote a rate for pets, and restaurants tend to be dog-friendly. Some public areas, like parks and beaches, may be off-limits for dogs.

YOU MIGHT SAY...

Do you have any pets?
Avez-vous des animaux de compagnie ?

Is it OK to bring my pet?
Est-ce que je peux emmener mon animal ?

This is my guide dog/assistance dog.
C'est mon chien guide d'aveugle / chien d'assistance.

YOU MIGHT HEAR...

I don't have a pet.
Je n'ai pas d'animal de compagnie.

I'm allergic to pet hair.
Je suis allergique aux poils d'animaux.

Animals are not allowed.
Les animaux ne sont pas autorisés.

VOCABULARY

farmer
l'agriculteur *m* **/ l'agricultrice** *f*

farm
la ferme

owner
le propriétaire / la propriétaire

fish food
la nourriture pour poisson

cat litter
la litière (pour chat)

barn
la grange

hay
le foin

straw
la paille

meadow
la prairie

flock/herd
le troupeau

guide dog
le chien d'aveugle

calf
le veau

lamb
l'agneau *m*

foal
le poulain

puppy
le chiot

kitten
le chaton

to walk the dog
promener le chien

to go to the vet
aller chez le vétérinaire

to farm (crops)
cultiver

to farm (animals)
élever

budgerigar
la perruche

canary
le canari

cat
le chat

dog
le chien

ferret
le furet

goldfish
le poisson rouge

guinea pig
le cochon d'Inde

hamster
le hamster

parrot
le perroquet

pony
le poney

rabbit
le lapin

rat
le rat

bull
le taureau

chicken
le poulet

cow
la vache

donkey
l'âne *m*

duck
le canard

goat
la chèvre

goose
l'oie *f*

horse
le cheval

pig
le cochon

sheep
le mouton

sheepdog
le chien de berger

turkey
le dindon

aquarium
l'aquarium *m*

cage
la cage

catflap
la chatière

collar
le collier

dog basket
le panier pour chien

hutch
le clapier

kennel
la niche

lead
la laisse

litter tray
le bac à litière

muzzle
la muselière

pet food
la nourriture pour animaux

stable
l'écurie *f*

alligator
l'alligator *m*

crocodile
le crocodile

frog
la grenouille

gecko
le gecko

iguana
l'iguane *m*

lizard
le lézard

newt
le triton

salamander
la salamandre

snake
le serpent

toad
le crapaud

tortoise
la tortue

turtle
la tortue marine

223

badger
le blaireau

bat
la chauve-souris

boar
le sanglier

deer
le cerf

fox
le renard

hare
le lièvre

hedgehog
le hérisson

mole
la taupe

mouse
la souris

otter
la loutre

squirrel
l'écureuil *m*

wolf
le loup

bear
l'ours *m*

camel
le chameau

chimpanzee
le chimpanzé

elephant
l'éléphant *m*

giraffe
la girafe

gorilla
le gorille

hippopotamus
l'hippopotame *m*

kangaroo
le kangourou

lion
le lion

monkey
le singe

rhinoceros
le rhinocéros

tiger
le tigre

blackbird
le merle

crane
la grue

crow
le corbeau

dove
la colombe

eagle
l'aigle *m*

finch
le pinson

flamingo
le flamant rose

gull
la mouette

hawk
le faucon

heron
le héron

kingfisher
le martin-pêcheur

lark
l'alouette *f*

ostrich
l'autruche *f*

owl
la chouette

peacock
le paon

pelican
le pélican

penguin
le manchot

pigeon
le pigeon

puffin
le macareux

robin
le rouge-gorge

sparrow
le moineau

stork
la cigogne

swan
le cygne

thrush
la grive

VOCABULARY

swarm
l'essaim *m*

colony
la colonie

cobweb
la toile d'araignée

insect bite
la piqûre d'insecte

to buzz
bourdonner

to sting
piquer

ant
la fourmi

bee
l'abeille *f*

beetle
le scarabée

butterfly
le papillon

caterpillar
la chenille

centipede
le mille-pattes

cockroach
le cafard

cricket
le grillon

dragonfly
la libellule

earthworm
le ver de terre

fly
la mouche

grasshopper
la sauterelle

ladybird
la coccinelle

mayfly
l'éphémère *f*

mosquito
le moustique

moth
le papillon de nuit

slug
la limace

snail
l'escargot *m*

spider
l'araignée *f*

wasp
la guêpe

woodlouse
le cloporte

coral
le corail

crab
le crabe

dolphin
le dauphin

eel
l'anguille *f*

jellyfish
la méduse

killer whale
l'orque *f*

lobster
le homard

seal
le phoque

sea urchin
l'oursin *m*

shark
le requin

starfish
l'étoile de mer *f*

whale
la baleine

VOCABULARY

stalk **la tige**	bud **le bourgeon**	bark **l'écorce** *f*
leaf **la feuille**	wood **le bois**	root **la racine**
petal **le pétale**	branch **la branche**	seed **la graine**
pollen **le pollen**	trunk **le tronc**	bulb **le bulbe**

YOU SHOULD KNOW...

In France, lily-of-the-valley symbolizes friendship, chrysanthemums are used as cemetery flowers, and yellow flowers can indicate jealousy.

FLOWERS

buttercup
le bouton-d'or

carnation
l'œillet *m*

chrysanthemum
le chrysanthème

daffodil
la jonquille

daisy
la pâquerette

hyacinth
la jacinthe

iris
l'iris *m*

lily
le lys

lily-of-the-valley
le muguet

orchid
l'orchidée *f*

pansy
la pensée

poppy
le coquelicot

rose
la rose

sunflower
le tournesol

tulip
la tulipe

PLANTS AND TREES

chestnut
le marronnier

cypress
le cyprès

fir
le sapin

fungus
le champignon

grapevine
la vigne

ivy
le lierre

lavender
la lavande

lilac
le lilas

moss
la mousse

oak
le chêne

olive
l'olivier *m*

pine
le pin

plane
le platane

poplar
le peuplier

willow
le saule

VOCABULARY

landscape **le paysage**	air **l'air** *m*	rural **rural**
soil **la terre**	atmosphere **l'atmosphère** *f*	urban **urbain**
mud **la boue**	comet **la comète**	polar **polaire**
water **l'eau** *f*	sunrise **le lever de soleil**	alpine **alpin**
estuary **l'estuaire** *m*	sunset **le coucher de soleil**	tropical **tropical**

LAND

cave
la grotte

desert
le désert

farmland
les terres cultivées *fpl*

forest
la forêt

glacier
le glacier

grassland
la prairie

hill
la colline

lake
le lac

marsh
le marais

mountain
la montagne

pond
la mare

river
le fleuve

rocks
les rochers *mpl*

scrub
les broussailles *fpl*

stream
la rivière

valley
la vallée

volcano
le volcan

waterfall
la cascade

cliff
la falaise

coast
la côte

coral reef
le récif coralien

island
l'île *f*

peninsula
la péninsule

rock pool
la flaque d'eau salée

SKY

aurora
l'aurore *f*

clouds
les nuages *mpl*

moon
la lune

rainbow
l'arc-en-ciel *m*

stars
les étoiles *fpl*

sun
le soleil

CELEBRATIONS AND FESTIVALS | LES FÊTES

"C'est la fête !" Everyone loves having a reason to get together and celebrate. In France, this usually means great food, the company of family and friends, and quite possibly a glass of champagne. In addition to the usual well-known holidays, there is also a wealth of French customs and traditions associated with the various holidays and festivals throughout the year.

costume
le costume

feather
la plume

mask
le masque

Congratulations!
Félicitations !

Best wishes.
Mes meilleurs vœux.

Well done!
Bravo !

Thank you.
Merci.

Cheers!
(À votre) santé !

You're very kind.
C'est très gentil de votre part.

Happy birthday!
Bon anniversaire !

Cheers to you, too!
À vous aussi !

Happy anniversary!
Bon anniversaire de mariage !

VOCABULARY

occasion **l'occasion** *f*	public holiday **le jour férié**	good/bad news **une bonne / mauvaise nouvelle**
birthday **l'anniversaire** *m*	religious holiday **la fête religieuse**	to celebrate **célébrer**
wedding **le mariage**	celebration **la célébration**	to throw a party **faire une fête**
wedding anniversary **l'anniversaire de mariage** *m*	surprise party **la fête surprise**	to toast **porter un toast à**

YOU SHOULD KNOW...

In France, as well as celebrating a person's birthday, it is also common to celebrate someone's name day ("la fête") – the feast day for the saint whose name they share.

bouquet
le bouquet

box of chocolates
la boîte de chocolats

bunting
les banderoles *fpl*

cake
le gâteau

champagne
le champagne

confetti
les confettis *mpl*

gift
le cadeau

funfair
la fête foraine

streamers
les serpentins *mpl*

There are 11 official public holidays per year in France. While these don't automatically shift if they fall on a weekend, it is commonplace to take an additional Friday or Monday off if the holiday falls on Thursday or Tuesday. This is referred to as "faire le pont" (literally "to make the bridge").

YOU MIGHT SAY/HEAR...

Is it a holiday today?
Est-ce que c'est un jour férié aujourd'hui ?

What are you celebrating today?
Qu'est-ce que vous fêtez aujourd'hui ?

I wish you...
Je vous souhaite...

And to you, too!
À vous aussi !

What are your plans for the holiday?
Quels sont vos projets pour les fêtes ?

Merry Christmas!
Joyeux Noël !

Happy New Year!
Bonne année !

Happy Easter!
Joyeuses Pâques !

Eid Mubarak!
Aïd Moubarak !

Happy holidays!
Bonnes fêtes !

April Fool!
Poisson d'avril !

VOCABULARY

baptism/christening **le baptême**	baby shower **la fête prénatale**	May Day **le premier Mai**
bar mitzvah **la bar-mitsva**	Mother's Day **la fête des Mères**	Valentine's Day **la Saint Valentin**
bat mitzvah **la bat-mitsva**	Father's Day **la fête des Pères**	Thanksgiving **le jour d'action de grâce**

birth **la naissance**	graduation **la remise des diplômes**	having a child **avoir un bébé**
first day of school **le premier jour d'école**	finding a job **trouver un boulot**	relocation **le déménagement**
passing your driving test **obtenir son permis de conduire**	engagement **les fiançailles** *fpl*	retirement **la retraite**
	marriage **le mariage**	funeral **l'enterrement** *m*

YOU SHOULD KNOW...

Bastille Day ("la fête nationale") is celebrated on July 14th to mark the storming of the Bastille in 1789 – an event that ushered in the French Revolution. It is usually marked with parades, firework displays, and lots of evidence of "le tricolore" (the French flag) being on display.

BASTILLE DAY

Bastille Day
la fête nationale

fireworks
les feux d'artifice *mpl*

garland
la guirlande

All Saints' Day
la Toussaint

April Fool's Day
le premier avril

Chinese New Year
le nouvel an chinois

Diwali
Dipavali *f*

Easter
Pâques *fpl*

Eid al-Fitr
l'Aïd-el-Fitr *m*

Halloween
Halloween *f*

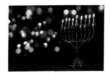

Hanukkah
Hanoukka *f*

Holi
Holi *f*

Mardi Gras
le Mardi gras

Passover
Pâque juive *f*

Ramadan
le ramadan

Christmas is usually celebrated on December 24th and 25th in France – many families have Christmas dinner just after midnight mass on Christmas Eve.

VOCABULARY

Christmas Eve
la veille de Noël

Christmas Day
le jour de Noël

Christmas card/tree
la carte / le sapin de Noël

New Year's Eve
la Saint-Sylvestre

New Year's Day
le jour de l'an

New Year gift
les étrennes *fpl*

YOU SHOULD KNOW...

Many French people send a New Year card ("la carte de vœux d'année") instead of Christmas cards. It's considered bad luck to wish someone a Happy New Year – "Bonne année !" – before the year is out!

Father Christmas/
Santa Claus
le père Noël

Christmas market
le marché de Noël

mistletoe
le gui

Nativity scene
la crèche de Noël

wreath
la couronne

Yule log
la bûche de Noël

Carnivals are usually held across France to celebrate Mardi Gras (literally "Fat Tuesday"), just ahead of Lent. The most famous of these is held in Nice, commonly believed to be the oldest carnival of its kind.

YOU SHOULD KNOW...

Carnival season gets underway with "la galette des Rois" (king cake), baked to celebrate the three kings visiting Jesus. This pastry is filled with frangipane, a sweet almond paste, and baked with a charm or "fève" (bean) inside it. The person who finds this is given the cardboard crown.

carnival float
le char

costume
le costume

effigy
l'effigie *f*

face paint
le maquillage

headdress
la coiffure

king cake
la galette des Rois

mask
le masque

parade
la parade

street performer
l'artiste de rue *m* /
l'artiste de rue *f*

ENGLISH

FRENCH

PHOTO CREDITS

Shutterstock: p19 timetable (Brendan Howard), p22 exterior below (JazzBoo), p31 minibus (Iakov Filimonov), p37 light railway (Bikeworldtravel), p37 porter (TonyV3112), p38 ticket machine (Balakate), p38 ticket office (Michael715), p38 tram (smereka), p38 validation machine (franticoo), p100 confectionery (Bitkiz), p103 cosmetics (mandritoiu), p103 food and drink (1000 Words), p103 footwear (Toshio Chan), p103 kitchenware (NikomMaelao Production), p103 toys (Zety Akhzar), p111 electrical retailer (BestPhotoPlus), p111 estate agency (Barry Barnes), p112 pet shop (BestPhotoPlus), p136 bureau de change (Lloyd Carr), p138 postbox (Alexandros Michailidis), p139 church (Ilya Images), p139 conference centre (lou armor), p145 sightseeing bus (Roman Sigaev), p147 carnival (Tory studio), p147 casino (Benny Marty), p147 comedy show (stock_photo_world), p148 musical (Igor Bulgarin), p148 opera (criben), p156 promenade (Oscar Johns), p160 choir (Marco Saroldi), p160 orchestra (Ferenc Szelepcsenyi), p173 football pitch (Christian Bertrand), p175 basketball shoes (Milos Vucicevic), p177 line judge (Leonard Zhukovsky), p177 umpire (Stuart Slavicky), p189 handball (Dziurek), p190 motor racing (Cristiano barni), p190 table tennis (Stefan Holm), p190 velodrome (Pavel L Photo and Video), p190 water polo (katacarix), p206 A&E (kay roxby), p213 labour suite (ChameleonsEye), p241 Bastille Day (DreamSlamStudio), p244 costume (Melodia plus photos), p244 headdress (LongJon), p244 parade (Capricorn Studio), p244 street performer (Kizel Cotiw-an). All other images from Shutterstock.

MICHAEL CRICHTON

CONGO

"Crichton is a master storyteller."
Detroit News

"*Congo* is so gripping that you almost expect Amy the gorilla . . . to bound into the room."
Christian Science Monitor

"Thrilling . . . [An] offering . . . to the mythology of a future so close and yet so unsettling."
New York Times Book Review

"Suspense that won't stop . . . A believable and immensely entertaining page-turner."
Houston Post

"A terrific novelist . . . He could make most readers lose sleep all night and call in sick the next day."
San Francisco Chronicle

"Michael Crichton isn't for scaredy-babies."
New York Daily News

BY MICHAEL CRICHTON

Fiction
THE ANDROMEDA STRAIN
THE TERMINAL MAN
THE GREAT TRAIN ROBBERY
EATERS OF THE DEAD
CONGO
SPHERE
JURASSIC PARK
RISING SUN
DISCLOSURE
THE LOST WORLD
AIRFRAME
TIMELINE
PREY
STATE OF FEAR
NEXT

Nonfiction
FIVE PATIENTS
JASPER JOHNS
ELECTRONIC LIFE
TRAVELS

MICHAEL CRICHTON

CONGO

"Crichton is a master storyteller."
Detroit News

"*Congo* is so gripping that you almost expect
Amy the gorilla . . . to bound into the room."
Christian Science Monitor

"Thrilling . . . [An] offering . . . to the mythology
of a future so close and yet so unsettling."
New York Times Book Review

"Suspense that won't stop . . . A believable and
immensely entertaining page-turner."
Houston Post

"A terrific novelist . . . He could make most readers lose sleep all night and call in sick the next
day."
San Francisco Chronicle

"Michael Crichton isn't for scaredy-babies."
New York Daily News

"Crichton is a virtuoso. . . . He can describe the look and feel of a rain forest as well as the latest safari gadgetry."
New York Times

"Michael Crichton is one of our most gifted popular novelists. A true son of Jules Verne and H.G. Wells, Crichton specializes in cutting-edge science fused with suspense . . . a master of plausible and frightening scenarios of science unloosed in the hands of the unscrupulous and the obsessed. He is a connoisseur of catastrophe."
Los Angeles Times

"Crichton is a doctor of suspense. Besides being an exciting saga, *Congo* is jam-packed with facts and knowledge about computers, technology, the jungle, and 'talking' apes."
Des Moines Register

"Michael Crichton has no peer at venturing off to the fringes of scientific research and dreaming up a yarn that will . . . frighten readers."
Orlando Sentinel

"Crichton has figured out how to package complex scientific, technological, and biological matters in ways that go down easy for the mass audience, and this is by no stretch of the imagination a bad thing."
Washington Post Book World

"Don't miss this one."
Pittsburgh Press

"Crichton knows how to craft a tale, one that keeps the reader turning the pages."
Houston Chronicle

"Intrigue-adventure . . . that really holds your interest."
New Orleans Times-Picayune

"The master of the high-concept techno-thriller . . . Crichton has a facile command for detail and for explaining complex technological matters in easy-to-grasp metaphors. . . . He has a knack for plotting at megahertz speed."
Chicago Sun-Times

"One of the great storytellers of our age . . . What an amazing imagination."
Newsday

"He marries compelling subject matter with edge-of-your-seat storytelling. . . . [Crichton] can thrill readers who love the heart-pounding chase. . . . He can impress techno-geeks eager to analyze the scientific data he weaves through his stories."
USA Today

"Crichton must have had as much fun writing this as his fans will in reading it. . . . Amy is a winner."
Publishers Weekly

"A splendidly proficient craftsman . . . The wellsprings of his curiosity [do not] run dry."
Washington Times

BY MICHAEL CRICHTON

Fiction
THE ANDROMEDA STRAIN
THE TERMINAL MAN
THE GREAT TRAIN ROBBERY
EATERS OF THE DEAD
CONGO
SPHERE
JURASSIC PARK
RISING SUN
DISCLOSURE
THE LOST WORLD
AIRFRAME
TIMELINE
PREY
STATE OF FEAR
NEXT

Nonfiction
FIVE PATIENTS
JASPER JOHNS
ELECTRONIC LIFE
TRAVELS